THE BEATITUDES

A STUDY SERIES

FRANK COLLIER

The Beatitudes
© Frank Collier 1994

ISBN 1 85852 026 6

INTRODUCTION

The Beatitudes are among the most familiar passages in the New Testament. But like many such well loved passages, they have attracted interpretations which are not always accurate. This is partly because the language of the early seventeenth century in the Authorised Version sometimes gives a false impression. For instance, the meaning of the word 'meek' was accurate enough as a translation in 1611, but today it has an association with weakness which is not what the Beatitude is about.

Moreover the people who listened to Jesus would have heard echoes of their own Scriptures. His words would have recalled verses from the Psalms and the Prophets as well as the books of Job and Proverbs which may be less familiar to us. In addition the teaching of the great Jewish rabbis is often recalled by Jesus' teaching.

It is possible to set the Beatitudes in the background of the Jewish Scriptures, and thus to illuminate the words of Jesus. It is also necessary to understand something of the intention of the writer of the first gospel. It is important to know why he recorded the Beatitudes in a different form to that chosen by Luke. It is also necessary to relate the Beatitudes to the Sermon on the Mount because Jesus was enlarging upon them in that sermon.

When we have done all this we shall find that the Beatitudes taken together give us a demanding outline of the qualities of the Christian character. They also face us with some practical challenges. Do they describe only very specially religious people, or can they describe very ordinary, everyday Christians? How do the meek survive in a world in which a macho brittleness appears to be the passport to fulfilment? How shall Christians with a passion for justice be satisfied in a world rampant with injustice? How shall we practice compassion in an increasingly harsh moral environment? Has the Christian enough authority to be an effective peacemaker?

Each study is followed by a series of questions. These should assist the leader in shaping discussion and help to stimulate the group. They could also help members of groups in preparing for the session. The notes and questions have been constructed together, so that the questions are not really an optional extra! You will not cover all of them in a session, but members may find it worthwhile to reflect on those that have been omitted at their own leisure.

I hope you will enjoy the studies.

Frank Collier
October 1994

1

SCHEME OF STUDY

SESSION 1

The Moral Teaching of Jesus

The Beatitudes describe the type of character, the tone and temper and quality of spirit, which makes for the coming of the kingdom . . . But having established this, we must go further. This ethical teaching is not merely ethical; it is essentially religious. Faith in God is the very nerve of it; cut that nerve and we shall have nothing left.

F. R. Barry, *The Relevance of Christianity*

Love is the general name of the quality of attachment and it is capable of infinite degradation and is the source of our greatest errors; but when it is even partly refined, it is energy and passion of the soul in the search for Good . . . Its existence is the unmistakable sign that we are spiritual creatures, attracted by excellence and made for the Good.

Iris Murdoch, *The Sovereignty of the Good*

Christian ethics and Christian faith

Thinkers who are unblinkingly aware of the twists and turns by which human beings satisfy their voracious egos, and who yet believe that we are spiritual beings 'made for the Good', are a rare breed. Iris Murdoch achieves that rare combination, and when she suggests that love is the energy and passion which gives power and stamina to the moral life, she seems very near to Christian belief.

Yet she is not propounding the secret of the Christian moral life. It is not enough to believe that we are spiritual beings. The secret lies in Christian faith. As Barry says 'cut that nerve and we have nothing left.' The morality of the Beatitudes and the Sermon on the Mount is the morality of a religious faith.

If at the very heart of all things there is a love which can never be extinguished or defeated, then we can venture on the kind of life which embraces gentleness of spirit, compassion, sincerity and peaceableness, and which is ready for sacrifice in the cause of justice and truth.

But if we are deceived and the predatory warfare of the natural world is all there is, then the future holds a dark prospect for the values of the Sermon on the Mount, and especially for the values of the Beatitudes.

Christian morality involves an immense leap of faith. The Sermon on the Mount begins and ends with that faith and so do the Beatitudes. This is constantly to be borne in mind as we seek to study them.

3

Jesus and the Jewish religious tradition

The role of Matthew

Some scholars believe that Matthew was being very selective in the Sermon on the Mount, and that he was emphasising the aspects of Jesus' teaching which appealed to his own traditional outlook. For instance, they point out that whereas Jesus in Matthew 5:17-19 emphasises that the Law must be kept in its entirety, he appears to have defied the law of the Sabbath, in particular by healing the sick. Moreover it is difficult to reconcile his direction to the disciples to heed the teaching of the Scribes and Pharisees (Matt. 23:2) with his fierce criticisms later in the chapter in which he condemns the Pharisees as blind guides (Matt. 23:24).

Yet although Matthew had an all too human tendency to emphasise what appealed to his own preconceived ideas, it is clear that the teaching of Jesus was centred in the Jewish religious tradition, and especially in the faith and teaching of the prophets. He also had a profound respect for the Jewish Law. This is what the evangelist stresses in Matthew 5:17.

The Law as a revelation of God

For Jesus moral precepts are the revelation of the character of God, and of the character which he demands of his children. This is expressed in the words 'Ye shall be holy as I am holy.' Jesus echoes this Old Testament command when he says 'Be ye therefore perfect, even as your Father which is in heaven is perfect' (Matt. 5:48). So not one dotted i or crossed t can be omitted from the Law because it is God's Law (Matt. 5:18).

Jesus was the last of a long line of prophets and teachers. They had all interpreted the Law, but Jesus made the unique claim in Matthew 5:17 that he was fulfilling the Law. He respected all those who had interpreted the Law, but set them on one side as 'those of old times'. He interpreted the Law, not simply in a new way, but with an authority which could never be set aside.

Jesus and the methods of the rabbis

The difference between Jesus and the Jewish rabbis is very important. The rabbis who interpreted the Law for the Jewish people believed that our character is determined by our conduct, and that if only a correct standard of conduct can be set up and enforced by law, men will become virtuous. So they believed that a strict law, severely enforced for everybody, was the first essential for God's people.

The Scribes tried to meet every eventuality by laws and regulations and succeeded in producing a body of legal prohibitions for the Jewish community. But they were often contradictory, difficult to understand, and an overwhelming burden for ordinary fallible human beings.

Today those who want to use the education system to enforce an agreed system of morals use the same argument as the Jews. From the point of view of communal moral health this may be an unassailable argument. As a means of securing the spiritual and moral wholeness of individuals it simply does not work.

4

Jesus started not with the law of the community, but with the individual. In his own words he came 'to seek and to save that which was lost' and his concern was with confused, spiritually hungry and often despairing men and women. He did not add to their burdens, but by his proffered friendship transformed the very essence of their outlook and behaviour. And in the Sermon on the Mount, by a series of pointed illustrations, he revealed to them just how this transformed life would express itself in daily living.

They would not simply respect the lives of their fellows, but their hearts would be free of hatred (Matt. 5:22). They would not simply be faithful in marriage; their minds would be free of lust (Matt. 5:28). They would not only love their friends but their enemies too (Matt. 5:43). Generosity would replace duty, and it would be genuine generosity, not a means of attracting a good reputation (Matt. 6:1-4). And their prayers and religious devotions would spring from love of God, not from a desire for the good opinion of their fellows (Matt. 5:5-18).

Jesus and the prophetic tradition

Jesus reached back to the prophetic tradition, to the need for an inner goodness that is perhaps best expressed in the yearning of Jeremiah when he dreams of a day when God will transform the human heart:

> But this is the covenant that I will make with the house of Israel after those days, says the Lord: I will put my law within theirs and I will write it on their hearts, and I will be their God, and they shall be my people.
>
> Jeremiah 31:33

So goodness comes as a gift of the Spirit of God, and the mind is freed from the kind of morbid self-examination which follows when men and women try to obey a detailed religious law. As Gunther Bornkramm aptly puts it, the Good Samaritan was not casting sidelong glances at God, but concentrating on the plight of the wounded man! His goodness was inbuilt.

This concern with the inner springs of human conduct does not mean that Jesus was not concerned with the evils of society, or with its injustices. What he knew, however, was that the changes which alleviate suffering and destroy oppression come from the dedication of those who 'hunger and thirst to see right prevail', from the sacrifices of the peacemakers and the compassion of the merciful. There is no social programme in the teaching of Jesus, but the Beatitudes themselves provide us with a catalogue of those precious characters who down the centuries have been agents of social transformation. The undying compassion of a Shaftesbury, or the inextinguishable moral stamina of a Wilberforce fit into this gallery of the blessed.

The blessings

To the Jews the whole Sermon, and especially the Beatitudes, must have seemed revolutionary. After all, they knew what the Blessing of God meant. It meant a long life, wealth and prosperity and good health. It meant a family of sons – the more sons the greater the blessing – and a good reputation in the community.

What then of Christ's blessings? Poverty, whether material or spiritual, had little to do with wealth. Sorrow did not fit into the picture of well being. Men and women who made themselves nuisances in the cause of justice, or interfered in private quarrels to try to bring about reconciliation were unlikely to be very popular. And the persecuted were unlikely to live long lives. Perhaps only compassion and purity of heart would seem qualities worthy of esteem in contemporary Jewish belief.

Nor can the Beatitudes be said to pour blessings on the successful men and women of the world. The thrusting and ambitious, the would-be rulers of nations and commerce, the leaders of armies and the agents of law and order would look askance at being told that the qualities expressed in the Beatitudes are of more account than their own merits. And I suspect that if you held an opinion poll on the qualities which the public wanted to see in their leaders, then those blessed by Jesus would not rank very commonly among them. This raises a number of important questions.

Some reflections

Whilst discussing the Beatitudes some months ago a number of Christian friends suggested that these qualities were natural ones, so that if you were born with a naturally volatile temper, it was little use expecting to find gentleness of spirit somewhere round the corner when you became a Christian. Peacemakers were people with a natural talent for effecting reconciliation. Even after mature reflection I still question this view. I believe it is possible, and indeed essential, that commitment to Christ means a transformation, gradual perhaps rather than instantaneous, but a transformation nonetheless, which endows us with qualities we otherwise would not have possessed.

Therefore we need to consider to whom Christ's words were addressed. Despite the presence of a crowd in the background, it would appear that Jesus was actually teaching his disciples, and the qualities are those which make for a dedicated Christian life. Manson in fact would firmly confine them to the Church:

> They are laid upon God's people as an unconditional obligation, as a distinctive mark whereby they are separated from all other people, and as a means whereby they may attain to their true blessedness.

If that is true, does it mean that to be a Christian a man or a woman must give up all hope of worldly success or even effectiveness in the community, that they must choose between, say, being members of Parliament and being Christians? Or does it mean that the Beatitudes were intended only for a small, almost monastic inner circle of devoted disciples, while the rank and file of average Christians toiled on in the world, soiling their hands and consciences in politics and business, but missing out on the greatest blessings?

Albert Schweitzer pointed his own way out of this dilemma. In 1910, in *The Quest of the Historical Jesus*, he advanced the view that Jesus had expected a final cosmic catastrophe within his own lifetime or as the immediate result of his own death. So the teachings of the Beatitudes and the Sermon on the Mount were only for a short term way of life for those who were soon to be his servants in the kingdom of God. Since the more worldly qualities would only be required of men for a very short time before the end of the present age, they were unimportant. The qualities of the kingdom of God would soon be established. To use the phrase of Schweitzer himself, the Sermon on the Mount was simply an interim ethic pending the imminent birth of the kingdom of God.

I prefer the interpretation of the great Hebrew scholar, T. H. Robinson, who points out that familiarity with the words of Jesus is apt to blind us to the force of his language. 'Blessed' is a Hebrew word which is really an exclamation, 'O the blessedness, the happiness of those who . . .'. Robinson goes on to suggest that Jesus is not offering rewards but stating facts. Sometimes he is describing a present blessing but sometimes one which lies in the future. 'He speaks as one who witnesses a great triumph or a striking success, and offers felicitations.'

So against all the odds we are here confronted with profound truths about life, which are relevant not just to the very devout, but to all who call themselves Christians. Perhaps the words of T. S. Eliot writing sixty years ago are still apposite. Writing under the title *The Strait Gate* he said:

> There is no good in making Christianity easy and pleasant; . . . even the humblest Christian layman can and must live what, in the modern world, is comparatively an ascetic life . . . You will never attract the young by making Christianity easy; but a good many can be attracted by finding it difficult, difficult both to the disorderly mind and to the unruly passions.

Certainly the Sermon on the Mount does not make it seem easy.

Questions

1. 'I don't mind being called to account for my actions, but my thoughts are surely my own.' This is one man's reaction to the Sermon on the Mount. Discuss.

2. If Jesus only intended the Beatitudes as an interim pattern for living, pending the end of the world, are they still valid for us?

3. 'The Beatitudes are inseparably linked to Christian commitment. They are not for the common man.' Do you agree?

4. Is the Sermon on the Mount a blueprint for a Utopian society?

5. Are the qualities blessed by Jesus natural or given qualities?

6. Discuss the view of Bornkramm that Christ does not expect us to live with a constant 'glance over our shoulder at God'.

7. At the end of the Sermon on the Mount it is recorded that the listeners noticed that Jesus spoke with authority. See if you can discern the secret of that authority.

8. Dean Inge once said that Jesus did not deal in 'Do's and Dont's', but rather said, 'Be a person of this kind of character.' Do you agree?

SESSION 2

The Sermons on the Mount and on the Plain

We possess no single word of Jesus and no single story of Jesus, no matter how incontestably genuine it may be, which do not contain at the same time the confession of the believing congregation, or at least are embedded therein.

Gunther Bornkramm, *Jesus of Nazareth*

The evangelists as interpreters

Before we turn to the Beatitudes in detail we need to understand their setting. In the Sermon on the Mount in Matthew's gospel, and in the Sermon on the Plain in Luke's there are two different versions. Most readers of the Bible are familiar with the version in Matthew, but less so with the abridged version in Luke. The differences are very important, because they show us that the evangelists were interpreters, not just recorders, of the words of Jesus for their churches.

The two sermons compared

If you read Matthew chapters 5, 6 and 7, and then Luke 6:20-49 you will find some close parallels, though the wording varies considerably. Roughly speaking the pattern is as follows:

Matt. 5:3	=	Luke 6:20
Matt. 5:6	=	Luke 6:21
Matt. 5:9	=	Luke 6:36
Matt. 5:10	=	Luke 6:22-23
Matt. 5:39	=	Luke 6:29-30
Matt. 5:44	=	Luke 6:27-28
Matt. 5:46	=	Luke 6:32-35
Matt. 7:1	=	Luke 6:37
Matt. 7:3	=	Luke 6:41-42
Matt. 7:15	=	Luke 6:46-47
Matt. 7:21-23	=	Luke 6:46-47
Matt. 7:24-29	=	Luke 6:48-49

The following have no parallel in the Sermon on the Mount:

Luke 6:24-26, 31, 38-40, 45

Outside Luke's Sermon on the Plain, there are parallels to Matthew's version in Luke 11 (Matt. 6:9-13) Luke 12:22-31 (Matt. 6:19-34) Luke 14:34 (Matt. 5:13) and Luke 16:17 (Matt. 5:18).

The evangelists have for the most part conveyed the same sense of Jesus' words, but have not preserved his sayings in his exact words. This is very different from the

Jewish practice which preserved the sayings of their rabbis exactly as they were uttered. This needs an explanation.

How the teaching of Jesus was transmitted

The Acts of the Apostles and the Epistles give the impression that there was little interest in the actual teaching of Jesus among the Gentile churches of Asia Minor and Europe. This may owe something to the preaching and writing of Paul, for whom the crucifixion and resurrection of Jesus were more important than his teaching. In fact, references to the teaching of Jesus are all but absent from Paul's epistles.

The Jewish Christian churches in Palestine, however, may well have cherished the words of Jesus, and so collections of his sayings, parables and other teaching began to be formed. Whether they were originally oral collections passed on by rote learning, or how soon they were committed to writing, it is impossible to say. It was one of those collections which provided Matthew and Luke with the material they have used in the passages we have noted above.

This collection, which scholars call Q, was almost certainly cherished in the church at Antioch, and may well have been taken there by Christians who fled from Jerusalem after the death of Stephen, when Saul of Tarsus conducted his fearsome persecution. So the origin of Q was very close to the events of Jesus' lifetime.

The passage of time may have caused variations to appear in the versions possessed by the local churches, or the two evangelists may not have considered it important to be exact in reproducing our Lord's words. What seems more likely is that the local churches themselves influenced the record. As F. R. Barry has pointed out, different circles of Christians each gave different interpretations of Jesus' sayings, according to their own experience. So Matthew's version probably records the response of Jewish Christians to Jesus' teaching, whereas Luke's version represents that of the Gentiles.

Both the experience of the churches and the personal convictions and purposes of the two evangelists played their part in giving us two different versions of the teaching contained in the Sermon on the Mount and in the Beatitudes.

Luke's version and its circumstances

The third gospel and the Acts of the Apostles, which were both written by Luke, were designed to tell a story. The gospel story told how Jesus of Nazareth was crucified as a result of a religious quarrel with the Jewish authorities. His death, however, was of greater significance for human beings than those brief facts would suggest. Jesus was the Son of God and by his resurrection from the dead, he set in motion a process which had led to the foundation of Christian Churches throughout the Mediterranean world. That process began with missionary work started by the church at Antioch, when it sent out Paul and Barnabas. And it was the spirit of that missionary movement which coloured Luke's writing.

Luke's gospel is the gospel of outreach, and shows Jesus embracing both outcasts and Gentiles. It is pre-eminently the gospel of forgiveness – the parables of the Lost Sheep, the Lost Coin and the Prodigal Son are all peculiar to this gospel. Above all it is the gospel of concern for the poor and needy and the Christian duty of love and care

9

for the poor is clearly taught. It is stressed in the teaching of John the Baptist as recorded by Luke, and it is not surprising to find him also recording that Jesus blessed the materially poor and the physically hungry. It fits the picture which is conveyed by the gospel, and especially by the parable of Dives and Lazarus (Luke 16:19-31).

The compassion of the evangelist, and possibly of the church of which he was a spokesman, does them credit. In days when we are ever more conscious of the plight of the poor and the hungry, and recognise the spiritual poverty which ensues from their material privation, we cannot but warm to Luke.

Nonetheless the two Beatitudes in Luke 6 raise a moral problem. Is it just or fair to promise suffering to rich people in a future life, simply because they were rich on earth? Is it just or fair to threaten those who enjoy a satisfactory diet with hunger in the next life simply because they 'never had it so good'? Neglect of the poor and hungry by the affluent is reprehensible, but there are generous rich people in the world, and wealth does not necessarily blind men and women to human need, though it may undermine their sensitivity. There is much to ponder here.

Luke's version of these two Beatitudes, however, has another possible explanation.

Dr. W. Manson has suggested that perhaps Luke misunderstood the words of Jesus. As a Gentile he may not have understood the significance which the Jews attached to the idea of 'the poor'. The Hebrew word for 'poor' describes godly and faithful people who have been the victims of ill-treatment and injustice.

For instance in Isaiah 41:17 the poor and needy, who are succoured by God, are the faithful remnant of the oppressed Jews in Babylon. Psalm 68, which is concerned with the oppression of the Jews, also promises God's goodness to the poor – the oppressed Israel (Ps. 68:10). These are but two examples of many to be found in the Psalms and the prophets.

Jesus may have been looking to a future in which Christians would be persecuted and oppressed, poor in the Old Testament sense, but blessed for their faithfulness. If that is the case, then Luke and the Gentile churches have interpreted the saying differently. Yet in view of verses like Mark 10:25, where Jesus emphasises how difficult it is for the wealthy to enter the kingdom of God, as well as parables like that of Dives and Lazarus, who is to say that Luke had not understood Jesus accurately?

Matthew and the Jewish tradition

The first evangelist was a Jewish Christian whose aim was quite clear: to show that Christianity was the true completion of Judaism. In spite of the rupture between Judaism and Christianity, caused by the rejection of Jesus, there had been a continuation of God's purpose in the coming of Jesus as the Christ. The three sacred possessions of Judaism – the Chosen People, the Temple and the Law – had simply acquired a new meaning. So Matthew used his deep knowledge of the teaching of the rabbis and his collections of Jesus' sayings to stress that continuity.

You will have noticed, for instance, how often he attached an Old Testament text to some episode in the life of Jesus in order to show that Jesus was simply fulfilling the prophecies about the Messiah. There is an early example in Matt. 1:18 where the birth of Jesus is connected with a prophecy from Isaiah, and these continue through the gospel.

He also showed that the very existence of the Christian Church was the fulfilment of the hopes of Israel. The Church is the new 'Chosen People'. In A. H. McNeile's words:

> The national privileges of the Jews had passed into the possession of the few who were true Israelites.

Matthew emphasised that Jesus had not undervalued the Law, but rather had regarded it as holy and by his teaching had fulfilled it (Matt. 5:17f). It was rather the Scribes and Pharisees who, by misinterpreting the Law and adding to it regulations devised by men, had been false guides to Israel and had prevented the Jewish people from being the ideal people of God that they might have been.

It is also probable that Matthew represented a section of the Jewish Christian Church who were somewhat alarmed by the immense preponderance of Gentile Christians in the churches of the Mediterranean area. Following Paul's lead, these Gentiles were apt to regard the Jewish Law as outmoded, its ritual obligations irrelevant, and only its moral demands to be respected. As a traditionalist among a very traditionalist people, Matthew was concerned that Christians should hold fast to their spiritual roots in the religious life of the Jewish people.

Questions

1. In the light of our conclusion that the evangelists have interpreted the words of Jesus, see how far you agree with the following statements:

   a) Realising that we are reading interpretations helps us to cope with differences in the recorded sayings of Jesus.

   b) It is helpful to have the evangelists' understanding of what Jesus meant.

   c) The interpretation gets in the way.

   d) Our understanding of the Bible is often inextricably bound up with the interpretations we have heard from teachers and preachers, or read in books.

2. Do you think that to bless the poor and to condemn the wealthy is acceptable as justice?

3. If Dr. Manson is right, many readers of St. Luke's gospel will get a false impression of Jesus' meaning. What practical helps are there available to prevent this?

4. What differences do you find in the picture of Jesus given to us by Matthew and Luke?

11

5. Matthew was anxious that Christians should not lose hold of their roots. Is it possible to be either too hidebound in our respect for tradition or to respect it too little in our attempts to speak the language of today?

6. Choose a passage from the Old Testament which you feel helps you to understand Jesus better.

7. 'Historically so difficult to get information about and when it is obtained, one who is apt to impress us so little alongside more than one founder of religions and even alongside many later representatives of his own religion.' This comment on Jesus was made by the eminent theologian Karl Barth. Do you agree with him?

Q - Quelle pronounced kell (German) Synoptic
Seeing together

M
Mk ⟶ Mt
Q ⟶ Lk
L

SESSION 3

Self-Knowledge and the Knowledge of the Kingdom of God

(i) The Meaning of Self-Knowledge

> More skilful in self-knowledge, even more pure,
> As tempted more; more able to endure,
> As more exposed to suffering and distress;
> Thence, also, more alive to tenderness.

William Wordsworth, *The Character of a Happy Warrior*

The Beatitude: Blessed are the poor in spirit, for theirs is the Kingdom of Heaven.

Various versions

The word here translated 'poor' literally means a beggar. In many countries today, even in our own, begging is an all too prominent feature of the life of teeming communities, and the poverty that necessitates it is all too pervasive. So when Jesus used the word it would conjure up a picture of abject poverty.

We have already seen that Luke and Matthew give a different version of these words. Modern translators do not vary much in their translation of Luke's words, tending to follow the Authorised version. J. B. Phillips, however, paraphrases it as 'How happy are you who own nothing', thereby emphasising the contrast with their ultimate possession of the kingdom of God.

Matthew's version is subject to rather more variation. Once more it is Phillips who seems furthest from the original. He translates it as 'How happy are the humble minded', which seems rather nearer to the meaning of meekness. The NEB introduces an element of self-knowledge: 'How blest are they who know that they are poor.' Moffatt has a similar rendering: 'Blessed are those who feel poor in spirit.' And it is that element which will give us the first key to our understanding of the Beatitude.

Luke's version

First of all, however, a brief reference to Luke's version. We have already discussed the possibility that Jesus used the word 'poor' to describe the persecuted and suffering Church. Here we must notice that Luke's compassionate concern for the abject poor and for suffering humanity has a significance for us. He felt that it was unjust that people should live lives of unrelieved poverty, oppression and ill-treatment, as well as suffering the ravages of disease. Surely in the final reckoning there would be some compensation for their unmitigated misery, and some punishment for their oppressors.

There is an echo of the cry of Amos:

> Here this, you that trample on the needy, and bring to ruin the poor of the land . . . The Lord has sworn by the pride of Jacob: Surely I will never forget any of their deeds.
>
> Amos 8:4, 7

The yearning for justice, which is so clearly seen in Amos, Micah and Isaiah has its counterpart in Luke's gospel.

Only a very insensitive Christian can observe without pity or anger the endless sufferings in Ethiopia, Somalia or the Sudan, where natural disaster leaving millions starving is made worse by civil wars and oppression. Nor can we contemplate without concern the extremes of wealth and poverty in the world at large. And most of us have known men and women whose lives have seemed to be an uninterrupted history of pain, grief and loss.

For the Christian, compassion for the sufferer must express itself in a longing for ultimate justice at God's hands. And perhaps part of the blessing promised is assurance here and now that God's justice will in the end prevail, simply because the cross proves that God cannot be defeated.

Matthew's version

Its antecedents

Matthew's version, too, is rooted in Old Testament ideas. For instance, in Isaiah 3:14-15 there is a promise of deliverance for the poor and needy, and punishment for an oppressive aristocracy because 'the spoil of the poor is in your houses.' Jeremiah 22:16 promises that God will judge the cause of the poor and needy, whilst Psalm 18:27 contains the assurance that God will 'deliver a humble people, but the haughty eyes you bring down.'

On the surface this does not look very different from Luke's compassionate yearning, but in the Old Testament the pious and devout, the faithful and the righteous were identified with the poor, the needy and the afflicted. Indeed, after the Exile the phrase 'poor and needy' almost always referred to the suffering Jewish nation.

Whatever Jesus himself intended, Matthew certainly regarded 'the poor in spirit' as referring to the body of the Christian Church, often poor materially, often suffering ill-treatment, but faithful and assured possessors of the kingdom of heaven.

Some interpretations

If we accept the translations of the NEB and Moffatt, which we noticed above, then the element of self-knowledge becomes important. But what kind of self-knowledge is implied? The poor in spirit are surely not the introverted who worryingly examine their motives and their responses to their human relationships, and emerge guilt-ridden and unsure. This would not be a state of blessedness.

The Old Testament again points us in the right direction. Numerous Psalms contrast our spiritual poverty and weakness with the abounding goodness of God. Psalm 103 must suffice to illustrate. It is shot through with gratitude for forgiveness, for healing, for protection, and renewal (v.1-6). Then the psalmist contrasts the goodness and the mercy of the Lord with human frailty (v.8-17). But the overall feeling that is conveyed is not one of gloom and guilt but of immense gratitude. It is this gratitude for all that we owe to God which is characteristic of the poor in spirit.

We may reflect that this is an altogether healthy attitude. We are more likely to bring to God a faithful service, if out of loving gratitude and in prayerful worship, we recognise honestly our follies and weaknesses, not hopelessly, but in the knowledge that the Father upon whose goodness we depend will renew us by his Spirit. Self-knowledge which is separate from our knowledge of a pardoning and restoring God can be psychologically dangerous and spiritually defeating. Indeed, some of the saddest people I have met have been those who dwell endlessly on feelings of remorse for moral failures, whether real or imagined, but without the liberating presence of a pardoning God.

I well remember a very able Christian lady who was obsessed by a moral failure which had occurred in her youth. She believed that God had forgiven her, but she could not forgive herself. She brooded over the past, and every human failing and inconsistency which she suffered was magnified into a deadly sin. She felt unable to serve in positions of trust in the Church despite her obvious aptitude. Perhaps more revealingly she felt often that she was not 'worthy enough' to pray. Instead of facing herself in the presence of a loving and forgiving God, her self-knowledge was derived from a barren soliloquy with herself. She was a tragic figure.

T. H. Robinson believed that, in this Beatitude, Jesus was emphasising the contrast between beggary and kingship. Here is a man who, by facing up to himself in the presence of God, has come to recognise those qualities which are of ultimate value. He knows that they cannot be purchased by wealth, or achieved by ambition, but that they are the fruit of God's leading through discipline and self-denial. The poor in spirit are those who take up the cross and follow Christ, and find sufficiency in the love of God which holds and directs them.

We are confronted with a challenge to our values. The kingdom of God is not reserved for those who understand New Testament Greek, for those with power and influence. It belongs to those who recognise that the greatest gifts in life are priceless. Faith can be the possession of an uneducated labourer, and love gives radiance to the life of an over-worked housewife. And the possessions which money or power or learning may bring are abject poverty without faith and love.

It is that quality which in the words of Bultmann, enables a man 'to decide for the demand of God which confronts him in the person of his neighbour'. The poor in spirit are ready to offer undivided loyalty to the God from whom they derive the real riches, and to share those riches with all who are in need.

The poor in spirit as people of prayer

I heard it suggested some years ago that the use of the word 'beggar' was a veiled reference to the necessity for prayer, and that the poor in spirit were people who lived by persistent prayer.

The beggar is utterly dependent on the generosity of the better off, and Jesus' parables about prayer in two cases emphasise that persistence in prayer, even despite apparent disappointment, is essential to the Christian life.

The neighbour who begs bread from his neighbour and friend at midnight provides a portrait of persistence. So does the woman who refuses to be put off by the busy judge, and pesters him until she receives a just settlement of her complaint. The exhortation to ask that we might receive, to seek that we might find, and to knock that the door may be opened to us, fits into the picture of the poor in spirit.

This has practical significance. It is easy to give up praying because our prayer does not seem to be answered. Our persistence in prayer is evidence not simply of our spiritual stamina, but of our capacity to receive and to value the blessing which we seek. Do we really want the blessing enough to persist? Have we really recognised its value? The genuinely poor in spirit know the value and persist in their prayers.

What is the kingdom?

It is impossible to answer this question fully and in detail because it could be the topic for a whole series of studies. But even a brief examination of what it means really does require a session to itself. So it must wait till next time.

Questions

1. Is there any sense in which Christians today could be regarded as 'poor in spirit'?

2. Think out some healthy practical steps by which Christians may reach self-knowledge.

3. Consider together some of the dangers risked by those who insist on self-examination without the help of the practice of prayer.

4. Look at the idea of gratitude and some of the benefits which it brings a) to our personal consciousness, b) to our fellowship with others. See if Psalm 103 helps your thinking.

5. A young friend of mine once said that love was the one great possession which no money could buy and was literally priceless. Do you agree with her or are there other possessions of even greater value?

6. Do your values find their origin in the New Testament, or are you greatly influenced by the values of the nation and community?

7. Does this Beatitude in any way help you to understand the practice of prayer more clearly?

SESSION 4

Self-Knowledge and the Knowledge of the Kingdom of God

(ii) The Blessing of the Kingdom

> The kingdom of God
> Is justice and joy,
> For Jesus restores
> What sin would destroy;
> God's power and glory
> In Jesus we know,
> And here and hereafter
> The kingdom shall grow.

Bryn Rees, *H&P 139*

It is difficult to cover this subject even in one whole session, but we can take a brief look at some of the implications.

The phrase 'Kingdom of God' was in common usage among the Jews. But Jesus transformed its meaning.

The Old Testament inheritance

The idea that God was the king of the people of Israel had a long history. Indeed, the idea that their gods were kings was not uncommon among primitive peoples. The idea is often found in the Psalms. For example, Psalm 95:

> For the Lord is a great God and a great king above all gods.

The same idea can be seen in Psalm 5:2, 10:16, 24:8 (God is the King of Glory) 47:7, 74:12, 98:6.

In the prophecy of Isaiah, however, the idea takes on the prospect of a future hope. In the opening verses of Isaiah 32 we have set before us the description of an ideal king who would be a refuge and a shelter for all who are in need: — *lovely reading.*

> See, a king will reign in righteousness, and princes will rule with justice. Each will be like a hiding place from the wind, a covert from the tempest, like streams of water in a dry place, like the shade of a great rock in a weary land. Then the eyes of those who have sight will not be closed, and the ears of those who have hearing will listen. The minds of the rash will have good judgment . . .

Thus the coming of this king appears to have a reforming effect on human character. The rash become prudent, and the hesitant confident. There is compassion and honesty in the administration of justice.

17

The familiar words of Isaiah 11 carry much the same idea. Here we are given a picture first of all of the ideal king, a descendant of David, and then of the ideal world which he will rule. The picture of the Prince of Peace in Isaiah 9 has a similar implication. *Note — His kingdom :*

The hopes of some Jews were very much centred on a worldly kingdom. God would establish a kingdom like that of David by sending his Messiah to drive out the Gentile oppressors, whether Persian, Greek or Roman, though the idea that God's people would become righteous, and that justice would be achieved, is also present.

In the centuries immediately before Christ, however, discerning spirits had begun to think of God's kingdom as more universal, embracing all men and women of whatever nation. This is reflected in the story of Jonah, where even the Babylonians, whom the Jews hated as oppressors, found a place in the love and purposes of God. It can also be seen in the beautiful story of Ruth from the country of Moab, who showed a loyalty and love which was an example to all Israelites. Moreover these discerning men and women did expect a transformation of human character much on the lines suggested by Isaiah.

So when Jesus came proclaiming the kingdom of God there were those who understood his mission in terms of a secular kingdom. But there were those, like Simeon (Luke 2), who had a quite different faith. It is that faith which is reflected in the words of this Beatitude as well as in the parables.

Jesus and the kingdom

There can be no doubt that the idea of the kingdom of God was at the very heart of Jesus' teaching. It is there in his first pronouncement (Mark 1:15). His healing is said to be a sign that the kingdom has come (Luke 11:20) and the kingdom is said to be in the midst or among them (Luke 17:21).

Moreover many of Jesus' parables present the challenge of the kingdom of God to his listeners. If they can respond with understanding and commitment to the qualities of mind and heart depicted by Jesus in the parables then they will come to know the secret of the kingdom of God. If, for instance, they admire the enterprise and commitment of the man who bought the land containing the hidden treasure, they may bring the same kind of commitment to the service of God.

The blessing of the kingdom

But what does Jesus mean here when he promises the kingdom of God to the poor in spirit? There are a number of questions we may ask.

First we may ask whether the possession of the kingdom is now or in the future.

Professor Fuller in *The Mission and Achievement of Jesus* placed the rewards which brought blessedness to the poor in spirit in the future. The poor in spirit must bear with their lowly condition in hope of a future blessedness. This was very much the understanding of the Beatitude current in the nineteenth century when stern Christians like Hannah More told the poor not to hope for betterment in this life. Their blessedness lay in the heavenly kingdom after death.

T. H. Robinson took the opposite point of view, claiming that the poor in spirit would have the present possession of the kingdom of heaven, because that poverty of spirit opened their hearts and minds to the riches of God's grace.

T. W. Manson felt that there is a paradox here. With the coming of Jesus the kingdom is already present, and men and women can experience its power, its peace and its joy. But its final fulfilment lies in the future, when the wrongs and suffering brought about by evil have been finally overcome. It is another way of saying what the fourth Evangelist implies when he speaks of people possessing eternal life here and now, although its full glory lies in the future.

Secondly we may note that the kingdom is the kingdom of our Father.

The promise of the kingdom is given in the words of Jesus: 'It is the Father's good pleasure to give you the kingdom' (Luke 12:32) and 'I appoint unto you as my Father has appointed to me, a kingdom' (Luke 22:29). This in no way undermines the authority of God, but it becomes the authority of a parent within a family, rather than the authority of the ruler of a secular state.

Thirdly we need to ask whether the kingdom is corporate or personal.

T. W. Manson has insisted that the kingdom cannot be conceived in any geographical or political sense. In fact Jesus was ruling out once and for all the older Jewish idea of God restoring a powerful secular kingdom like that of David. It is 'a personal relation between the King and the subject'. It is essentially spiritual. He goes on to interpret this as meaning that those who possess the kingdom are conscious of the protection and guidance of God.

It is important to grasp this last statement. There is a secular parallel in our nineteenth century history. A British citizen in one of the Greek islands had been maltreated by the Greek authorities. Lord Palmerston, then Prime Minister, made a speech in the House of Lords in which he described a Roman citizen's rights. For a man to claim that he was a Roman citizen would bring the whole power and might of the Roman empire to his assistance. Palmerston claimed that if a man said, 'I am a British citizen' the whole power and might of the British empire should similarly come to his assistance. It was a somewhat pompous speech, but in the spiritual world the Christian, as a citizen of the kingdom of God, may likewise rely confidently on the resources of that kingdom.

Such confidence is obviously a moral and spiritual possession. Christians are not exempt from the accidents, calamities and personal illnesses which afflict our fellows, nor from errors of judgment. If I foolishly get too near to a fire, the fact that I am a Christian will not protect me from burning. Or if I attempt a jump which is beyond my capability, my Christian belief will not prevent my breaking a limb. I am just as likely to visit my local hospital as my agnostic neighbour. I may face suffering with greater inward calm because of the grace of God, but I am subject to every necessity of my human condition.

So it is in the realm of moral choice that the protection applies. I have myself sometimes discerned a moral protection which has operated at critical times, when a particular choice might have entailed moral danger. Either the door has closed, taking away the possibility of a wrong decision or action, or the conscience has been singularly sensitive and defensive of my moral integrity.

The fellowship of the kingdom

Yet the kingdom surely cannot be exclusively a matter of a personal communion with God. Jesus himself speaks of the kingdom in terms of joyous festal occasions, weddings and feasts, and the present experience of the kingdom of heaven must surely include the joyous experience of love within the family of God.

Partly for this reason in the Middle Ages the Church and the kingdom of God were identified together in Catholic thinking. The keys of the kingdom had been given to Peter, and his spiritual descendants as Bishops of Rome held the same authority. So the Church was the embodiment of the kingdom of heaven on earth.

I believe that the fellowship of the Church is not the same as the kingdom of God, but that it points to the fellowship of the kingdom of God. The kingdom embraces the Church, but is infinitely greater in its universality and scope. The Sacrament of the Lord's Supper is a symbol of that family fellowship and bears witness to the fellowship of the kingdom still to come.

David Jenkins, the former Bishop of Durham, has also taken a wider view of the kingdom of God. In his book, *God, Jesus and the Life of the Spirit,* he points out that the suffering of Jesus deals with everything that is in contradiction to the kingdom: sin, disobedience, destruction and death. 'God is at one with us. Love is the power of the kingdom, triumphing by taking it all on.' So love cannot be defeated. Here perhaps is an answer to that yearning which we noticed in Luke's version. God bears the injustices of our world through Christ's death and resurrection, and his love in the end will be greater than any justice we can yearn for or expect.

Conclusion

I have been helped by comparing the kingdom to the experience of rock climbing. Climbers are securely roped to each other and to their skilled and confident leader. They are bound together in the risks and perils of their climb. Self is lost in comradeship. Loyalty to each other takes precedence even over personal safety. Trust and obedience to the leader alone lead to achievement and to security. Is not this the relationship of Christians to each other and to Christ? And is not the kingdom a saving fellowship?

Here then is the source of confidence for the poor in spirit. They are aware of the presence of God, who underwrites all the risks and adversities they may suffer, by the suffering love of Christ. In the words of Lady Julian of Norwich, they have the confidence that, 'All shall be well and all manner of thing shall be well.' This is no empty optimism or groundless idealism, but the fruits of their experience of being open to the grace of God.

Questions

1. Do you think that life is generally unjust? Do you believe that God will finally secure justice for his children?

2. Do you think that the kingdom of God is simply a personal relationship between yourself and God, or a set of relationships of which God is the centre?

3. In what way do you understand a) God's protection, b) God's guidance?

4. Does it make any difference when we think of the kingdom of God as the kingdom of our Father?

5. 'All shall be well and all manner of thing shall be well.' In our contemporary world have we that confidence?

6. Does the fact that monarchy is so different today from that of the ancient world make it difficult for us to understand the blessing of the kingdom of God?

7. Which of Jesus' parables help you most to understand what he means by the kingdom of God, and how does that relate to the 'poor in spirit'?

SESSION 5

In the Shadow of Grief

> Grief fills the room of my absent child
> Lies in his bed, walks up and down with me
> Puts on his pretty looks, repeats his words,
> Remembers me of all his gracious parts,
> Stuffs out his vacant garments with his form
> Then have I reason to be fond of grief.

Shakespeare, *King John*

The Beatitude: Blessed are they that mourn, for they shall be comforted.

The experience of grief

Grief is the experience which touches everyone. It is inseparable from the fact of death. I have heard the loss of a partner or child described as almost as painful as a physical amputation. The grief expressed in the instance quoted above is testimony to its power. The mother of Prince Arthur finds memories afflicting her in a perverse way. The joy of his company, his attractive appearance, his childish words, even his clothes tear at her emotions. Shakespeare has expressed the devastation by which one-time joys become piercing grief.

The Beatitude is an almost incredible paradox. Who could set side by side the grief of losing a child with the joy of birth? Or who could speak in the same breath of the ecstacy of love fulfilled in marriage with the death of husband or wife? The exclamation, 'Oh how happy are those who mourn' is by far the hardest Beatitude to accept.

Grief is not only confined to bereavement. One of the most grief stricken women I ever met was a mother whose son had just received a prison sentence. She said that prison was almost worse to contemplate than his death might have been, because at least in death she would have unspoiled memories. Now she was caught between the horror of what he had done, and the love which she felt for him despite his crime. And she was constantly tormented by a terrible sense of the waste of a capable and educated young man. This was mourning indeed.

An older generation of Christians was apt to interpret the verse as referring to grief for sin, and indeed it is possible for a person to be grief stricken for wrongs committed, especially where the person who has suffered is dead. Thomas Hardy spent months touring the places which were associated with his first wife, and wrote poems expressing his grief, largely because he regretted that he had not treated her more thoughtfully and caringly when she was alive.

John Wesley gives the impression sometimes that he understood the Beatitude in this sense and that it implied 'godly sorrow for sin'. The verse is, of course, general

22

enough to be open to that interpretation, but I am inclined to think that Jesus was speaking of sorrow in all its aspects rather than this rather narrow version of it.

Grief and love

At the heart of this Beatitude is one incontrovertible fact. Grief is inseparable from the experience of love. S. R. Lysaght expressed this thought in a remarkable poem:

> If love should count you worthy, and should deign,
> One day to seek your door and be your guest,
> Pause ere you draw the bolt and bid him rest,
> If in your old content you would remain;
> For not alone he enters; in his train
> Are angels of the mist, the lonely guest
> Dreams of the unfulfilled and unpossessed,
> And sorrow, and Life's immemorial pain.
> He wakes desires you never may forget,
> He shows you stars you never saw before,
> He bids you share with him for evermore
> The burden of the world's divine regret.
> How wise you were to open not! and yet,
> How poor if you should turn him from the door!

We can only experience love if we are ready to accept pain and grief and loss.

How desperately we try to separate the two! If we have loved deeply and unreservedly and have been hurt badly in consequence, we do not easily give ourselves in unreserved love again. We put a rampart round our feelings, so that in the event of loss the hurt is minimised. In the process of course we lose out, because in anaesthetizing ourselves against possible pain, we also dull our capacity for the joy of love, and our relationships are tepid, insecure and often doomed from the outset. Such is the common human experience.

But to draw back from the commitment of unreserved love because it may occasion pain and grief is to draw back from God. God is love and 'he that dwelleth in God dwelleth in love,' caught up in that love which in Christ is seen to be suffering love. Only if we are prepared for his grief can we share in his love. That is a startling and sometimes unwelcome realisation, but it is the inescapable truth. The Beatitude blesses the sorrowing because all who dwell in the love of God must experience the sorrow of the cross.

Mourning then and now

Societies older than our own had traditions of formalised mourning. The Jewish world of the Old Testament took mourning very seriously. The book of Wisdom in fact enjoins devout Jews to 'weep for the dead, so as not to be evil spoken of'. This would take the form of intense wailing and beating of the breast. Often there would be fasting, and almsgiving to the poor as an act of both gratitude and grief.

Although Christian mourning rites were much modified by the hope of eternal life, and the belief that one day there would be a joyous reunion in heaven, the Church

23

never escaped entirely from older traditions of mourning. In some countries today Christian mourning can be as pronounced and demonstrative as that of the Old Testament.

Many will be disposed to welcome the disappearance of formalised mourning in our own society. We probably should not regret the disappearance of the over-expensive funeral which sometimes landed poorer people in debt, or the wearing of black for months afterwards and the keeping up of an appearance which only the most intimate members of the family actually felt.

However, formalised mourning had its value. It helped to express grief in a way which was socially acceptable. Today there is a danger of much suppressed grief. Whilst people may be expected to shed tears, there is sometimes impatience with those who do not quickly cast aside their grief, and look towards the future. 'Life has to go on' is a common expression. 'Business as usual' on the part of the bereaved is regarded as a sign of strong character. In fact, unexpressed grief is psychologically damaging.

Perhaps the advent of bereavement counselling, valuable and essential as it is, is nonetheless a sign that in an age which has banished formalised mourning and has little religious belief to put in its place, our society is finding it difficult to cope with grief.

Comforting the mourner

In the absence of religious comfort, other consolations are offered. A sudden death can be described as 'a nice way to go', without prolonged pain and despite the shock to the family. Death after a long and painful illness can be described as 'a blessing'. Both consolations have a basis in fact, but the Christian has more to offer, and so has the Beatitude.

The central belief of the Christian Church is that Christ, by rising from the dead, 'brought life and immortality to light through the gospel'. So for the Christian the foundation of all comfort ought to be the hope of eternal life. The belief that there will in due course be a reunion with those we have loved in the kingdom of heaven was for centuries the light that shone out in the darkness of grief. Indeed the sorrows and suffering of this life were seen as a brief prelude to the joy of heaven. A twelfth century hymn says it all:

> Brief life is here our portion,
> Brief sorrow, short lived care;
> The life that knows no ending,
> The tearless life is there.
> O happy retribution!
> Short toil, eternal rest;
> For mortals and for sinners,
> A mansion with the blest.

Yet I sometimes wonder how far that hope remains part of the Christian comfort for many apparent Christians. For some at least belief in an after life is very vague. Some feel that all we can know of eternal life is the experience of God's love here and now in this life. On the fringes of the Church there are those who have been drawn

24

away to a belief in reincarnation which certainly has no foundation, either in the New Testament or in the doctrines of the Church. Perhaps we need to be better schooled in our beliefs.

How did Jesus face grief? We read that he was deeply distressed by the death of Lazarus (John 11:35). The Upper Room on the eve of the Crucifixion must have been dark with grief because of his realisation that his disciples lacked the loyalty and trust to meet the exacting demands of the moment, and that his betrayer was there with him. His words to the disciples show that he believed that God would transform that dark time into a means of grace for the disciples, and for all who sought his Table through the centuries. Their very discouragement could be transformed into a source of power.

Similarly in the Garden of Gethsemane he found comfort in his grief through his inherent trust in God, and the grief at seeing his own people seeking to destroy him was met with a clinging to his Father. In the end he could believe that his work had been accomplished. Only that unbroken communion with God which had characterised his life could have carried him through such grief when, for a time, the very presence of God seemed lost to him.

There is a pointer here for us. If, in our days of peace and contentment, we have been open to God, we may hope that in the darkness of grief we will be able to feel that the Christ who knew what it was to be 'a man of sorrows and acquainted with grief' is one with us. And because he is one with us, God is one with us too. That is surely the meaning of the Beatitude.

Questions

1. Think together about some of the diverse effects of grief on people. How can faith help to counteract those effects?

2. In what ways do you think the Church ought to support those in grief, both in the Church and in the community? Think especially of those who suffer the grief of broken marriages, children spoiling their young lives, as well as those who are bereaved.

3. Are love and grief inseparable? If so, is there a temptation to be reserved in our love, and what effect does it have upon our relationships?

4. Do you think that the disappearance of formalised mourning is altogether a good thing?

5. How does the hope of eternal life fit into your beliefs? Is it a comfort? If not, can you point to any other source of comfort in grief?

6. Discuss the sources of comfort that Jesus found in his own grief.

SESSION 6

Meekness – Virtue or Folly?

But the meek shall inherit the earth; and delight themselves in abundant prosperity.

Psalm 37:11

Too often Christians have preferred the heathen worship of the stronger virtues to the Christian ideal.

J. S. Banks, *Hastings Dictionary of the Bible*

Better is it to have a small portion of good sense with humility, and a slender understanding, than great treasures of science with vain self-complacency. Better is it for thee to have little than much of that which may make thee proud.

Thomas a Kempis, *The Imitation of Christ*

The Beatitude: Blessed are the meek, for they shall inherit the earth.

Versions and readings

The Greek word which here is translated 'meek' is not common in the New Testament, and where in the epistles we find the English word 'meek', the Greek words differ according to the writer. The Latin Bible (the Vulgate) follows this, using one word in Matthew 5, but words which have slightly different associations elsewhere. Thus in Paul's epistles to the churches, the idea of humility and modesty is emphasised. In the epistles to Timothy and Titus it is gentleness, and in James it is teachability.

Modern translators have opted for the idea of gentleness of spirit, though Phillips speaks of the blessing being for those who claim nothing, a translation which is apt to leave a feeling of a rather vapid character, rather than the strength of character which we see in all genuinely gentle men and women.

The roots of the idea of meekness are in the Old Testament, especially in the Psalms and in the prophecy of Isaiah. In fact the Beatitude itself is practically a quotation from Psalm 37:11. The promise that God will save and protect the meek is found in Psalm 76:9 and 147:6, whilst Psalm 22:26 is almost a parallel to Psalm 37:11 when it speaks of the meek 'eating and being satisfied'.

A well known passage in Isaiah 11 speaks of the Messiah vindicating the meek who are oppressed, and the equally well known passage in Isaiah 61, which Jesus read in the synagogue at Nazareth, speaks of the servant of God bringing good news to the meek. And although the word 'meek' is never used, the picture of God's servant in Isaiah 42:2-4 is of one of gentleness and strength, which combined together are the essence of meekness. We can see, therefore, that Jesus' hearers would be well acquainted with the idea of 'the meek'.

The nature of meekness

It is important to dissociate the idea of meekness from weakness. Meekness does embrace gentleness, kindness and forbearance as against a proud, harsh and unforgiving spirit, but in no sense does it mean the kind of character which through fear or timidity would yield to the superior force of a bullying or obstreperous person. Meekness is a sign of strength.

The apostles obviously valued meekness. Paul pleads with his readers to practice meekness (Eph. 4:2 and Col. 3:12). He numbers it among the fruits of the Spirit (Galatians 5:23). Both Titus and Timothy are instructed to deal gently with their people (1 Tim. 6:11 and Titus 3:2). James speaks of meekness as being a sign of wisdom.

Yet as J. S. Banks has said, Christians have been torn between the qualities of gentleness and humility and the virtues of courage, endurance and assertiveness. It is not difficult to see why. The Middle Ages were a time of insecurity and internecine war, when the military virtues were in high demand. The Church chose to give its blessing to the Crusader and to the gallant knight, because this seemed the surest guarantee for the survival of a Christian society.

Later on Luther blessed the German princes and the qualities which seemed to make for strong, peaceable states. And modern national churches have become the spiritual arm of the nation state. Meekness is not a quality readily associated with political power, however desirable some rulers may find it to be in their subjects!

Yet as we shall see the quality of meekness is not just a requirement of Christian living, it is part of the necessary spiritual equipment for our place on this planet.

Inheriting the earth

There are two contrasting strands in the Old Testament. On the one hand there is a belief that man was intended by God to dominate the world:

> You have given them dominion over the works of your hands; you have put all things under their feet, all sheep and oxen, and also the beasts of the field, the birds of the air, and the fish of the sea, whatever passes along the paths of the seas.
>
> Psalm 8

This sense of lordship has carried through into the Christian era.

On the other hand the Jews shared with other ancient peoples a belief that inordinate pride, or what the Greeks called 'hubris', would be mankind's downfall. It implied that human achievement was at the centre of the world's life and showed people meddling with concerns that were God's. The story of the Tower of Babel is a primitive example. So is the story of King Uzziah who, in arrogant disobedience, burnt incense in the Temple, a task reserved for the priests (2 Chron. 26:16-18). The prophets often speak of God punishing such pride. This insight is what lies at the basis of the Beatitude. Today when we consider human mastery of the planet and human technological achievement as of prior importance, we are guilty of hubris. Some Christians might consider that genetic experiments are also a form of hubris.

27

We need a much more humble attitude to nature and to the planet on which we live, as well as towards human life itself.

In 1939 T. S. Eliot wrote an essay which could equally well have been written in 1994:

> We are being made aware that the organisation of society on the principle of private profit as well as public destruction, is leading both to the deformation of humanity by unregulated industrialism, and to the exhaustion of natural resources, and that a good deal of our material progress is a progress for which succeeding generations may have to pay dearly.

He went on to mention such disasters as soil erosion. Had he been still alive, he would probably have mentioned rain forests and the ozone layer. What is important, however, is his strong conviction that a wrong attitude towards nature implies a wrong attitude towards God. He went on:

> It would be as well for us to face the permanent conditions upon which God allows us to live upon this planet . . . We have yet to learn that it is only by an effort and a discipline greater than society has yet seen the need of imposing upon itself, that material knowledge and power is gained without the loss of spiritual knowledge and power.

It is perhaps worth noting that Francis of Assisi, the saint whose reputation for meekness is almost a byword, was also the saint of whom stories are told about his remarkable rapport with animals and birds. He is also the author of a hymn (HP 329) which expresses the comradeship of man with nature. His prayer, 'Make us channels of thy peace' is the expression of his personal meekness and gentleness. And although we do not often meet people of his stature, we do meet men and women who bring to the natural world a humility, a readiness to learn and a respect for the world's creatures and their habitats which should shame us. Perhaps the meek are the only ones whom God can trust to inherit the earth.

Meekness in relationships

Meekness is more obvious in human relationships than in relationship to nature, and its absence is even more damaging.

Here is a businessman, a churchman whose son has become a leading consultant surgeon of immense dedication. Yet the father can find no joy in his son's work because he had set his heart on the boy taking over the family business. His love is tarnished by his desire to run his son's life. He is not meek in the biblical sense. Or there is the teacher who is affronted because her star pupil turns to other studies for her academic career. Her genuine care for her pupil is marred by a desire to dominate the girl's decisions. Even a minister can fail in meekness when young people whom he has cherished begin to think for themselves, and perhaps begin to look at their faith in a way of which he inwardly disapproves.

Service to God can be equally marred. Dorothy Sayers in her play, *The Zeal of Thine House*, tells the story of the twelfth century builder William of Sens who built part of Canterbury Cathedral. He was a proud man and was so overcome by that pride that it became more important to him that he should complete the part of the building he had planned and achieve fame, than to serve God. In his arrogance he attempted a dangerous operation and fell. He was crippled and unable to complete his work. And we do not need to be famous builders to spoil our service to the Church by a failure in meekness, a self-centred hunger for praise and recognition.

Too much Christian service and genuine care can be shot through with self. Yet it is possible to find many who are ready to take that second or even third place and find joy in it, even though they would have dearly loved the post of great responsibility.

Meekness means that the people we serve and the spirit in which we serve are more important to us than our own self-importance or public reputation. The New Testament contains one very moving example in John the Baptist, who could say of Jesus, 'He must increase and I must decrease.' He was ready to accept his place as the forerunner, and also to accept that with the coming of Jesus his work was done. The strength of the disciplined prophet showed in this expression of meekness.

The serenity of the meek

Meekness often shows most clearly in the serenity of a person of gentle spirit, and that goes hand in hand with a spiritual stamina, which enables such people to endure much suffering and privation, and carry out long and frustrating tasks with calm and unflustered competence. This shows very clearly in Jesus himself. He could be angry, as he was in the Temple courts, when he saw the exploitation of poor people by money changers and merchants. He did not mince his words when confronted by hair splitting and prevarication. He was critical of hypocrisy. He must have been frustrated by the slowness of his disciples. He was often tired. But there was always a serenity which made him immovable.

T. H. Robinson has summed it up:

> To the ordinary mind, it is the aggressive, the self-confident, the self-asserting, the self-advertising who win their way in the world and gain the earth for themselves. The humble man is in all respects the exact opposite of this, and it is he who, as Jesus sees, will ultimately inherit the earth. The capacity for submissive endurance will in the long run prevail over dominant aggressiveness.

Years ago I saw the truth of this with my own eyes. There lived on a large housing estate in Hull a devoted Christian woman, the wife of a docker. She was a gentle person, quietly spoken, with a welcoming presence and home. Her prayers showed her to be very close to Christ, but it was in her relationships that her serene bearing and inner peace showed most. She had an ear for her neighbours' troubles. She could comfort youngsters who sought her home in their distress. She could take the strain during a local bereavement. And miraculously she could halt a bully in his tracks without lifting her voice. She could calm an irate church business meeting and shame us into penitence. I never read the Beatitude which we have been studying here without thinking of her. She was strong in her utter selflessness and glorious in her gentleness. She was already blessed.

Questions

1. Do you think that it is true that Christians are not ready to be meek?

2. Is meekness a primary Christian virtue?

3. How do we reconcile the apparent need for intensive production to maintain standards of living with a right attitude towards nature and its creatures?

4. Look at the examples given above, where genuine service has been marred by the desire to dominate, and find examples where quiet unselfishness has been much more effective.

5. Serenity is a Christian quality. Is it the natural endowment of some people, a gift to those who have faith, or is it achieved by personal self-discipline?

6. Find examples of the meekness of Jesus and discuss how it worked and its effects on people.

7. Meekness is confused with weakness. Look for the ways in which there is strength in meekness.

SESSION 7

The Quest for Righteousness and Justice

Fiat justicia et pereat mundus – Let justice be done, though the world perish.

The Emperor Ferdinand I (1506-1564)

What doth the Lord require of thee but to do justly, to love mercy and to walk humbly with thy God?

Micah 6:8

The Beatitude: Blessed are they that hunger and thirst after righteousness, for they shall be filled.

Versions

Phillips and Moffatt substitute the word 'goodness' for 'righteousness'. This is not simply a concession to modern usage, but implies an inner health of spirit rather than an outward conformity to moral or religious laws. The NEB, however, introduces a hint of social righteousness and of justice:

> How blest are those who hunger and thirst to see right prevail; they shall be satisfied.

Both these translations are important. They reflect the emphasis which Jesus laid upon the obedience of heart and mind rather than outward conformity to a set of rules. Additionally the NEB captures the Jewish meaning of the word righteousness, which was always likely to be in the mind of Matthew.

The prophets and righteousness

Once more we need to go back to the Old Testament. E. W. Heaton has pointed out that, for the Jew, righteousness was not a duty imposed by religion; it *was* religion, the way, that is to say, of knowing and serving God. He goes on to say:

> Basically the term 'righteous' means that which is regarded as being standard and normal. Thus for example, it was used to describe 'just' or standard weights and measures. To be 'righteous' means, therefore, to conform with the accepted standard, to be 'in the right'.

Thus it was as important to be right in observance of the rituals of the Temple, which were essential to the welfare of an agricultural and trading community, as it was to be faithful in marriage, to treat one's neighbour 'rightly' and to be scrupulously honest in buying and selling. To be righteous was a legal requirement, the consequence of belonging to the people of God, and as enforceable as the legal responsibilities of British citizenship are today.

The Beatitude is undifferentiated, and standing by itself it could simply confer God's blessing on those who struggled to keep the Law in every little detail, in other words the Scribes and Pharisees. But Jesus insists that the righteousness of his disciples should surpass that of the Pharisees, and the remainder of the Sermon on the Mount makes it clear that Jesus was following the prophetic tradition. He was concerned not with outward righteousness, but with that inward obedience to God which we noticed in Session 2. On another occasion he actually quoted from the prophet Hosea, pointing out that God wanted compassion and not sacrifices. It is this kind of righteousness for which the blessed have a passionate concern.

The Puritan tradition

It is very easy for religion to fall away from the ideal of personal communion with God into a routine matter of maintaining a conventional pattern of life. No one should deride conventional good living, for the health of any community depends upon it. But it does have many pitfalls.

For example, dissatisfaction with their 'worldly' fellow Christians leads the zealous to try to fasten very stringent moral demands on the lives of the well meaning and decent. So the zealous hedge the life of a nation about with regulations, mostly of a negative and forbidding kind. This happened in the seventeenth century in Britain and in the Netherlands. The Puritan domination in Britain was at its height during the period between the death of Charles I and the accession of his son in 1660, when Cromwell, the titular leader of the nation, and rival parties of zealots strove to make England a righteous nation.

Socially the ultimate effects were calamitous. The nation tired of restriction, and the sixty years that followed the accession of Charles II were some of the most licentious in our history. Perhaps that should teach us that it is impossible to compel men and women to accept a Christian morality for which they do not possess the basic faith. The attempt to do so is usually counter-productive.

Economically, however, it has to be admitted that the repression which the Puritan middle classes accepted in the name of their religious faith released energies which helped to build up a mercantile and financial empire second to none in the world.

But the spiritual cost was considerable. Both here and in the Netherlands the passion for righteousness bred a hard, proud and unforgiving spirit. Only look at seventeenth century Dutch paintings like Rembrandt's *The Night Watch* and you will see the stern, unbending pride of very self-righteous men. Turn over the pages of the story of the New England colonies and find the heretic hunting and crusades against witchcraft, which caused suffering to many innocent men and women. This quest for righteousness is not the quest which was blessed by Jesus. It is far more reminiscent of the obsession with the Law which characterised the Pharisees.

The evangelical tradition

At the time of the Reformation the quest for righteousness was answered by Luther in quite a different way. Luther placed no value on human righteousness, not just an outward show of it, but all righteousness and wisdom of ours, however sincere and heartfelt they might be. He claimed that all human righteousness makes us complacent and self-centred. In the words of Philip Watson:

> Even the best and sincerest of men who have pursued righteousness 'from a sheer passion for virtue' with never a thought of making a boast of it before others, have not been able to prevent themselves from being inwardly pleased with themselves and glorying in it at least secretly in their hearts.

In that case, to seek righteousness with passion, as the Beatitude suggests, can only be done by ceasing to strain and struggle after moral goodness. We must simply cast ourselves upon God, that our faith may be the means whereby the righteousness of Christ saves us from our sins and is implanted in our hearts.

We may recognise that Christian righteousness is a gift rather than an achievement, the fruit of the Holy Spirit in our lives. Our faith gives us such a sense of being accepted by God in Christ that we can trust him in our temptations, make our decisions when we are puzzled by life's dilemmas with a quiet confidence, and discover that we are sharing his love with others in our relationships.

If you are familiar with the Epistles of Paul, you will find that Luther is a theological bedfellow of the apostle. Paul declaimed against the righteousness of the Law as fervently as Luther declaimed against all human goodness. Whether Matthew, when he recorded the words of Jesus, would have understood them as Paul and the evangelicals do, is another matter. Certainly if you read the Parable of the Sheep and the Goats (Matt. 25:31-46) you will be left with the impression that God values all compassionate concern for our fellows and all loving service.

There are those today, however, who would say with Luther that human goodness has no value in the eyes of God because inevitably it is marred by our sins, and at best leads us into pride and self-satisfaction. So to hunger and thirst after righteousness is to seek Christ in faith that he may satisfy us with his righteousness.

We are left with the unanswered question, if we are honest. Does God not value even the humble struggling goodness which falls over its own sins, but which derives from an honest and good heart? Having met people who manifest that kind of goodness I find it hard to believe that Christ would not look upon them as kindly as he did upon the Good Samaritan.

The quest for justice

If we take the reading of the NEB, which we quoted at the outset of this study, then the blessing is intended to apply to those who have a passion for social justice, which includes a passion for being personally fair in their own dealings. As T. H. Robinson says:

> To be fair is one of the most difficult of achievements and only those who have a real passion for justice, who feel that their very souls will perish without it, have any real chance of attaining it. But given that passion they will be satisfied.

Once more the quest for justice was a central theme in the preaching of the prophets. Amos and Micah cried out for justice for the poor. Ezekiel and the second Isaiah promised justice for an oppressed Israel.

In the East at the time of Jesus there was much to arouse such a passion because, for the poor, justice was hard to come by. Nor is it difficult to identify such passion in Christian history. The anti-slavery movement, the campaign for the reform of prisons, the struggle against apartheid, to mention only three great movements, have featured men and women who were prepared to sacrifice any personal happiness and contentment in the struggle. Nothing could have priority over that concern. And there is much in our present world and national situation today to arouse that passion in Christians, if we keep ourselves informed. Justice is still at a premium in our world.

Terence Rattigan in his play *The Winslow Boy* gives expression to the passion for justice by what, for me, is a parable. A lad is expelled from Dartmouth Naval College allegedly for forging a signature on a postal order. He denies the offence, and his family believe him. A distinguished barrister, brought in to clear his name, also believes in his innocence. Together they launch a campaign through the courts and in Parliament. The cost is enormous. The family's finances are ruined. The health of the parents deteriorates. An older sister loses her chicken-hearted fiance. The barrister loses his chance of political preferment. The nation's affairs are interrupted. But as the barrister says, if the time ever came when the affairs of Parliament could not be interrupted by a matter of justice for a little boy and his postal order, then something vital would have been lost for the nation.

It sounds very old fashioned in its high sounding idealism, but one would like to think that it could still be true. The recovery of the passion that right shall be done would be a sign of recovered health in our society, at least as important as our economic output.

Christians who are concerned for social and racial justice are not generally popular, even among their Christian contemporaries. They are told that they should not meddle in politics. Trevor Huddleston was often given this advice in South Africa. He pointed out that sin is not just a personal matter, but that evil affects the whole human race. And of the Old Testament prophets he said:

> Half of their time was spent in trying to bring home to men of their day the fact that God was directly concerned in the way society was organised; in the way wealth was distributed; in the way men behaved to one another. In short – politics.

When the Church hungers and thirsts after right then it needs to heed the example of Amos, Micah, Isaiah and Jeremiah. It has a prophetic tradition to maintain and a message as challenging as theirs to deliver.

Moreover, justice in society is a necessary foundation if ordinary men and women are not to lose their incentive for their own moral lives, and to lose faith in their own moral values. As the American writer Walter Lippmann said in his *Preface to Morals*, life today is 'a field for careers, an arena of talent, an ordeal by trial and error and a risky speculation'. He believed that the fortunes of men had come to bear no relation to their merits and efforts and so, 'the God of the modern world is Luck.' Before men and women will become passionately concerned about their own personal goodness, they will have to feel that the life of the world, and of their own society in particular, bears more obvious signs of the justice which is so often demanded of them.

So where do those with a passionate hunger for justice find the satisfaction which is here promised to them? Often the quest must seem a losing struggle. If the achievement of justice is the source of the blessedness which Jesus promised, then many may feel that the promise simply does not work. The scales seem to be weighted against them. Some will be able to look back on the history of the fight against injustice, and say that in the long term the fight brings results. Just occasionally an injustice is brought to light, and an aroused public opinion causes the perpetrators to retreat. But it is often beyond the brief lifetime of those who are engaged in the struggle.

The life of Martin Luther King offers a rather different picture. Slandered, attacked with violence by vicious enemies, and eventually assassinated, there was little to show at his death that his struggle would be effective in the short term. Yet I have rarely seen the film of his last great oration, with its powerfully reiterated confidence – 'I have a dream' – together with its premonition of an early death, without feeling that he was satisfied because of a God-given assurance that the dream was a future reality. Perhaps this is the meaning of the blessing – that those who are nearest to the front line in the battle against injustice are also nearest to God and to his abiding righteousness and love.

Questions

1. Some religious bodies, including Islam and the Roman Catholic Church, where it is in a majority, believe that the state ought to enforce morality as well as punish crime. How far do you feel that morality is a personal matter in which the state ought not to interfere?

2. Is it right to expect people who do not share our Christian faith to accept our moral teaching?

3. In the twenties a strong anti-drink lobby resulted in Prohibition in the USA. The outcome was an underground network of drink smugglers who became the gangs of later years. What lesson can we learn from this?

4. What value do you place, and what value do you think God places, upon ordinary human goodness regardless of religious faith?

5. T. H. Robinson said that it is very difficult to be fair. Why?

6. We honour those who fought against injustice in the past. But the crusader of today is often regarded as a troublesome crank or positively hated. Why?

7. Is goodness a gift or an achievement?

8. From where do you think satisfaction comes to those who hunger and thirst after justice?

SESSION 8

The Quality of Mercy

For mercy has a human heart
Pity a human face
And love, the human form divine
And peace the human dress.

William Blake, *To Mercy, Pity, Peace and Love*

The Beatitude: Blessed are the merciful, for they shall obtain mercy.

The meaning of mercy in the Bible

T. W. Manson has pointed out that there is a parallel with this Beatitude in the teaching of the Jewish rabbis. One such text reads:

He who has mercy on his fellow men receives mercy from heaven.

This is another example of how the teaching of Jesus would strike a chord for those who were familiar with the teaching of the great rabbis, even though Jesus often turned these sayings in new directions.

This saying is also a forceful example of the way in which the language of the Authorised Version in English has ceased to give the correct impression. When we think of mercy we think of forgiveness, of the reprieve of a convicted criminal, or the sparing of prisoners in wartime. The Hebrew word *hesed* does include mercy in those senses, but it has a much wider meaning. T. H. Robinson explains this:

Hesed is the perfection of that mystical relation of one personality to another which is the highest of all possible grades of friendship. It means a sympathetic appreciation of other persons, the power, not merely to concentrate blindly on them, but to feel deliberately with them, to see life from their point of view.

He goes on to point out that *hesed* applies to the relationship between God and man as well as between human beings. Finally he emphasises that if we translate the word either as love or mercy, we must remember that it includes not merely emotion but also intelligent sympathy.

In the Old Testament *hesed* is only used twice to mean forgiveness, both in the book of Deuteronomy (21:8 and 32:43). Usually it is used to signify a relationship of intense loyalty, such as that which existed between David and Jonathan.

In this study we shall first of all examine the wider meaning of mercy and then look at the more familiar idea of the relationship between divine and human forgiveness.

Mercy as compassion

The word compassion suggests itself as a good translation here because it literally means 'feeling with', or in our modern language 'fellow-feeling'. The intelligent sympathy which Robinson insisted upon is evoked by compassion.

Pity is often easier to come by. Compassion is a costly exercise. In the first place it is not easy to enter fully into understanding the point of view of other people, unless we already share some affinities. A Westerner may want to understand what it feels like to be an underprivileged person with a black skin. But the very attitudes of anger and resentment, of inability to trust more privileged people, and the position of economic inequality, may well prevent the black man from any personal disclosure. And that can apply to underprivileged people of the same nation.

Educational inequalities can be just as frustrating. A person may not have the word power to express either his feelings, or to describe his true needs. He may not even understand them himself, much less be able to communicate them. If in addition he feels as if he is under a social microscope, he may not even show himself as the person who deep down he really is.

Psychologists too have found that the kind of relationship we have with people often determines what we can actually learn about them. Ask three teachers to give a profile of a particular pupil, and you will often be astonished by the differences which appear. Indeed it is sometimes difficult to recognise the same pupil in the three accounts. The reason is that the pupil's response to the teacher will depend on their relationship. If there is a good rapport, he is likely to reveal far more of his true self. This applies to all human relationships. It means that we can only have true compassion if we are ready for a genuine relationship of mutual trust and loyalty with people, and that can only happen where there is equality of respect.

Some years ago I was fascinated to watch a television programme about the work of a group of American scientists in an Indian community. They were trying to help the people to improve their crops, and to raise their general standard of living, building and furnishing their homes in greater safety and comfort, and guarding against disease. It was noticeable that the Americans were good listeners. They did not overwhelm the villagers with sound advice. They were ready themselves to profit from what they learned from the local people. They treated the venture as a partnership – what we as Christians would call fellowship. There was obviously a remarkable degree of mutual trust and even of affection. There was compassion, but it was not pity, rather genuine fellow feeling.

This Beatitude, then, calls us to relationships of humble sharing rather than a condescending pity, however much the condition of our fellows may move us.

The way of forgiveness

The narrower understanding of mercy with which we are familiar is not easy to accomplish. It is not always easy to forgive without giving an impression that we are condoning an offence. A husband or wife or child may interpret forgiveness as either weakness or moral indifference. A pupil may equally misunderstand the pardon of a teacher. So genuine forgiveness is taxing. In the effort to make our abhorrence of the wrong understood we may give an impression of condescension, which simply cancels

37

out the forgiveness. We are seen as martyrs, and resented as such. We have failed to restore a broken relationship.

Nor is it easy when we are badly hurt to reach out in a forgiving spirit. Where onlookers have been aware of the humiliation and have pitied us, their reaction may well be at the back of our minds. Humiliation eats at self-respect, and erodes a merciful spirit. The deeper our love for the offender, the more sharply we feel the betrayal. And how difficult it is to enter again into the trusting relationship which forgiveness implies. We may forgive but can we forget?

In contrast with this uneasy acceptance of the duty of forgiveness stands Jesus' manifest joy in forgiving. The picture of the shepherd seeking the lost sheep reveals no reluctance to embrace the sinful person. The father of the prodigal son does not hold a conference with himself to determine an appropriate attitude to his new found son. His embrace is the natural expression of uncalculated, loving pardon. As Jesus encountered men and women burdened by guilt, he emulated the figures in his parables by his own free forgiveness. This is the pattern for our own forgiveness of others.

How different is the picture that Shakespeare presents in *The Merchant of Venice*. Here a calculating Portia counsels mercy in poetic terms to Shylock, who at the hands of his Christian neighbours has never known mercy. They have wronged him, and he craves revenge. The pound of flesh which he seeks from Antonio is the harsh penalty for years of arrogant contempt. Portia knew that the appeal would go unheeded. Mercy might befit the 'throned monarch better than his crown'; it might be 'an attribute of God himself'. But it was too much for Shylock.

Here in exaggerated form is the calamity which long remembered grievances inflict upon society. Vengeance has to be forsworn if Shylock is to escape the loss of his daughter, the loss of his money and the loss of his religious faith. He is broken as are so many unforgiving individuals and communities. Long histories of brooding on past wrongs erupt in the destruction of innocent lives in Ireland, in Africa, in the former Yugoslavia. A world without forgiveness is unthinkable, but the word vengeance is written larger on the pages of world history than the word mercy. Nations and communities, even churches, find it as hard to forswear retaliation for past injuries as Shylock himself.

Perhaps for this reason we are often at our most unforgiving as individuals when our offended dignity is entangled with strong political or religious convictions. Naturally kind and generous people who would forgive a personal wrong are apt to demand harsh penalties for crime. Paul, who was a loving friend to his churches, found it hard to forgive Mark when he returned home during the first missionary journey. He thought that the young man had betrayed the cause. I can remember instances where there were bitter relationships between churches where one had been created by a secession from the first half a century before. So difficult is forgiveness when thwarted by religious passion.

Yet forgiveness is just as essential where great matters of state or of faith are at stake. Brooding over long remembered grievances has already led to the strife which has afflicted Ireland and Eastern Europe. Vindictiveness and stiff necked pride are not capable of social healing.

The unforgivable

No one can mistake the connection between readiness to forgive and the promise of forgiveness. Manson puts it very clearly:

> The man who cherishes an unforgiving spirit against his neighbour proclaims by that the fact that his own repentance is not genuine, and that he is himself therefore unforgiveable, unfit to receive God's forgiveness.

This is the theological expression of what is an unhappy truth. It sounds unduly formal and rigid, but the condition exists nonetheless.

In one of his lesser known works, *The Great Divorce*, C. S. Lewis describes in fantasy how a man and woman who have died are on their way to the Judgement Seat. They encounter a well known convicted murderer, who appears to be an emissary from heaven. The man is appalled and affronted to find the murderer in heaven. What right has a criminal there?

His immediate reaction is to set off indignantly to claim his rights for his own blameless life. The murderer begs him to pause. All he will receive is love freely given. He has no rights. The man brushes aside the advice angrily. He only wants his rights, he does not want bleeding charity. Quietly the murderer says, with a clear reference to the passion of Jesus, 'Bleeding charity! That is exactly what you will get.'

The man had never understood forgiveness. He had never sought mercy from other people. Perhaps he would have felt humiliated to do so. Nor had he felt it necessary to be forgiving. All men should have their just deserts. We can imagine him as a harsh judge of his fellows, and quite unprepared to look at life from their point of view. As a result he was unforgivable because he was incapable of understanding forgiveness.

There are probably few people so extreme that even a chink of light cannot illuminate their hearts. But if we catch ourselves mentally condemning a fellow being to some harsh punishment, or reflecting that someone does not really deserve our kindness and generosity, then we should pause and consider the words of Portia:

> Though justice be thy plea, consider this
> That in the course of justice none of us
> Should see salvation: we do pray for mercy:
> And that same prayer doth teach us all to render
> The deeds of mercy.

Questions

1. How difficult is it to have fellow feeling with people whose background and experience is different from our own, especially if they turn out to be not very likeable?

2. Is it possible deliberately to forge a loyal relationship with other people?

3. Which should take priority in our thought and action, justice or mercy? Does it make a difference when we think of ourselves as individuals or as citizens?

4. Carefully consider why forgiveness is taxing to those who forgive.

5. If you had been Portia how would you have treated Shylock?

6. Sometimes Christians are more unforgiving to fellow Christians who fall away from high standards and are subject to church discipline, than they would be if the man or woman hurt them personally. Are they justified?

7. Is the object of justice to punish or to rehabilitate?

8. Can any person be totally unforgivable?

SESSION 9

The Transparent Christian

An honest man's the noblest work of God.

Pope, An Essay on Man

Remark all these roughnesses, pimples, warts and everything as you see me, otherwise I will never pay a farthing for it.

Cromwell's instructions to the painter, Lely

The Beatitude: Blessed are the pure in heart, for they shall see God.

Living in the presence of God

All religions have concepts of purity. To come into the presence of a god has always been considered dangerous for anyone who was 'impure'. That word included ideas which would seem strange to us. For instance, a person with a physical flaw, or disabled in some way would be excluded from worship by some primitive religions, and diseases like leprosy were considered particularly impure. In some religions, too, women were considered to be impure. In the Jewish Temple a woman could not come too close to the holiest place. It was also a serious matter to undertake religious rites when one had been in contact with a dead body, for example, or attended a birth where blood had flowed.

The Old Testament

There are signs of this in the earliest parts of the Old Testament. But by the time of Amos, Micah and Hosea the idea of purity had become moral, and it was the purity of right living which they emphasised. 'Be ye holy for I am holy' had a moral ring to it.

Both the Psalms and the prophets stress the purity of God himself. Thus Psalm 12:6 says:

> The words of the Lord are pure words; as silver tried in a furnace of earth, purified seven times.

Psalm 19 is more familiar:

> The commandment of the Lord is pure, enlightening the eyes.

Familiar too is the vision of God's holiness in Isaiah 6 where the prophet shakes with fear, because he himself is unclean or impure and in the presence of God that must be dangerous. That vision touches the heart of the Old Testament belief that to be in the presence of God one must be pure.

41

So Micah can ask:

> Can I tolerate wicked scales and a bag of dishonest weights? Your wealthy are full of violence, your inhabitants speak lies, with tongues of deceit in their mouths.
>
> Micah 6:11-12

Moral purity is imperative in the presence of God. Psalm 73 speaks with both assurance of God's favour to the pure and of the danger of impurity:

> Truly God is good to the upright, to those who are pure in heart. But as for me, my feet had almost stumbled; my steps had nearly slipped.

The Psalms also often contain prayers for purity. A familiar petition is in Psalm 51:

> Create in me a clean heart, O God, and renew a right spirit within me.

The New Testament

Outside the Sermon on the Mount, the concept of purity is not frequently mentioned. In Philippians 4:8 the word pure simply means chaste. In the Pastoral Epistles, 1 Tim. 3:9 and 2 Tim. 1:3 the word describes a good conscience. In James 1:27 it means faultless and is nearer to the moral ideal of the Old Testament. Only in 1 John 3:3 is the need for the worshipper to purify himself mentioned, and there the content of the rest of the epistle shows that the need is for purity from hatred and ill will.

A question of motive

The most obvious reading of the Beatitude is one that connects it with the remainder of the Sermon on the Mount. Those men and women whose motives are beyond reproach will be blessed with a vision of God. We touched on this in Session 2. We noticed that it is necessary to be free from hatred as well as to abstain from killing. It is necessary to be free from lust as well as to avoid adultery. Honesty must be heartfelt. Generosity must be sincere, and not aimed at public approval. Prayer and fasting must have a sincere intent.

This is a demand for a moral life of a very high order. I remember a very earnest Christian saying that while she could control her actions, thoughts and desires often rode into her mind unbidden. Nor could she guarantee that she was unaffected by the good opinion of others, or that she did not enjoy a little praise and encouragement. Don't we all?

Certainly only divine grace could effect such a profound selflessness in most of us. If the implication of the Beatitude is that we must be totally pure, only God himself can effect such refining. The most sensitive Christians are all too conscious of unworthiness when they worship and pray, and only the faith that they will not be cast out by a loving and forgiving God enables them to live in his presence.

The test of sincerity

There is, however, another possible interpretation of the Beatitude. Phillips translates thus:

Happy are the utterly sincere, for they will see God.

You will have noticed above that sincerity both in generosity and in religious devotion is important in Jesus' teaching. So Phillips' translation has support in Matthew 6. Moreover, Jesus is very sharp in his criticism of hypocrisy in other parts of the gospel, notably in Matthew 23.

The gospel picture

Hypocrite is a Greek word meaning a person who wears a mask, as actors did until modern times. So a hypocrite is a person who is insincere, and whose outward actions are really simply acting and are not matched by genuine inner feelings.

In the gospels hypocrisy seems to blind men and women to the truth that Jesus is the Son of God. In fact the Beatitude may well be not just a promise for the future, but a statement about the present. It is the utterly sincere people who recognise Jesus. Simeon holds the child Jesus in his arms with joy. Nathaniel, the 'Jacob without Jacob's cunning', is quick to confess his faith in Jesus. They are prepared to be seen for what they are, sinful human beings with many faults, and so they see Jesus for what he is – the Son of God.

By contrast the Pharisees cannot believe what they see. In Luke 11 we are told that they started a rumour that Jesus was healing by the power of the prince of devils, Beelzebub. They saw the power of health and sanity being given to people, and they attributed it to evil. And the root cause of this moral blindness was hypocrisy. They wore a mask of piety which all too often concealed motives and desires that conflicted with their outward profession. As Jesus said, they looked for the praise of men rather than the praise of God. And so, because they knew inside themselves that they were insincere, they could not believe in the transparent goodness of Jesus. Perhaps those whose lives are a hypocritical act are, of all people, the most precluded of all from finding God in Jesus.

The situation today

Is there then a connection between our contemporary inability to recognise goodness and honesty when we see it, and the inability of the majority of people to recognise the lordship of Christ? I suspect that there is. There is a cottage industry today, devoted to the single aim of discovering the flaws of character, the psychological imbalance, the so-called sins of those who have been given the respect and admiration of their fellows. No one can devote himself to a great cause like Martin Luther King did, without becoming the target of an undermining process which seeks to destroy his character by imputations of scandalous behaviour. The heroes of yesterday are dissected and proved to be fraudulent. No one is worthy of our reverence or respect, for everybody is a hypocrite. This is the gospel of the late twentieth century popular media.

The public read and enjoy the scandal, partly because they find it titillating, but also because they know that they are themselves not what they seem. They are putting on a social act a great deal of the time. But there is no need to feel any shame, because even the great and the good have their guilty secrets.

Of course, there is a sense in which only half consciously we all wear masks. We like people to approve of us, and so we present an appearance which we think pleasing. We feign an interest in what people are saying, when we are actually bored. We express joy or sorrow which we only partly feel. We seek to impress people with our achievements or our connections. We lie to avoid having to face an embarrassing situation. In the process our capacity to enjoy genuine goodness is spoiled, and I suspect that our capacity to find God in our dealings in daily life, as well as in our worship, is undermined.

Years ago J. B. Priestley, in a play entitled *Dangerous Corner*, advanced the view that insincerity, even lying, is a social necessity. A group of friends at a house party begin to play a game which involves telling the truth. One person rashly reveals her knowledge of a love affair between two of the others. Once that truth is out, other damaging exposures follow in quick succession, until, at the climax, a murder takes place. Then, in typically Priestlian fashion, we are shown that all this was a fantasy, showing us what might have happened had the woman really told the truth as she was tempted to do at the 'dangerous corner'. By inference we are advised that social peace depends on hiding the truth, on insincerity.

In the seventeenth century Moliere, in *Le Misanthrope*, tackled the same subject in a different way, presenting a character who was so scrupulously honest that he refused to flatter people, refused to hide his true feelings about them, and behaved in what was regarded as a boorish fashion. He lost his friends and his intended bride because of his unwillingness to pretend to feelings and thoughts which he did not hold.

Politicians often claim that it would be impossible to govern a country if they always told the truth, if they were always sincere in their promises and their undertakings. Deception is part of the business of gaining power and maintaining it. A civilisation so flawed is unlikely to have clear lines to its spiritual foundations – to be open to God. What is true for the insincere individual is also true for the community which has lost its taste for truth.

A biblical test case

The test case in the gospel is to be found in Mark 12. There a group of Scribes and Pharisees demand of Jesus from where he derives his authority. What will his answer be?

He tests their honesty. Can they tell him from where John the Baptist derived his authority? Immediately they are in conference. They sense that if they acknowledge that John was indeed a prophet sent by God, then Jesus will ask why they did not heed John's words. On the other hand, if they deny that John was a prophet, they will offend the people who revered him. So they refuse to answer, pleading ignorance. They are being fundamentally insincere and dishonest. So, with complete justification, Jesus refuses to answer them, knowing full well that if they lack the moral courage and sincerity to answer him, they will not have the moral integrity to accept his answer.

Perhaps the acid test of our own purity of heart comes when we seek an answer to our prayers, or search the Bible for some deeper understanding of God's ways. Sometimes before we can find the answer, we are challenged to confront our own condition, to acknowledge some cherished sin, to seek to heal some broken relationship, to accept some responsibility which we have shirked. We hide from the sin, blame the bad relationship on the other person, and find excuses for evading the responsibility. Then we complain that God has failed to answer our prayer, that try as we will we cannot find the deeper understanding that we seek. God is silent because we have proved that we lack the purity of heart to recognise and accept his answer. To be open to God requires sincerity and honesty courageously expressed in our prayers and in our fellowship.

A cautionary tale

G. K. Chesterton in a Father Brown story, *The Arrow of God,* tells the story of a priest, who was accustomed to ascend his church tower to pray. He had a dissolute brother whose behaviour was scandalous, and one day whilst at the top of the tower, he saw the brother in the street beneath him. Hatred and disgust filled his heart, and in a moment of unbridled anger he threw down a stone which killed the brother. So, says Chesterton, though he was a good man he committed a great crime. Had he been praying where he should have been, in the church below amid ordinary sinful and needy people, it would not have happened. He was looking down on a sinful world, not sharing its burdens and its needs.

There are few people so intolerant as those who are self-righteous. Purity of heart always carries in its strength the qualities of compassion, of mercy and of love. We find Jesus always among those who have the greatest need, and if we would recognise him, it will be because we realise how utterly right it is that God should be with the lost and the bewildered, the hopeless and the oppressed. The purity of heart which has to retreat from contact with ordinary, vulnerable human beings, and which finds its only contentment in a cloistered virtue, will never know blessedness. The truly blessed are those arresting men and women whose sincerity and openness is so transparent that goodness shines out from their lives, even though they work and serve among corrupted, often morally ugly people. You see, the refining quality which gives purity is not isolation, but love.

Questions

1. Is it possible to have entirely pure motives, free from selfish concerns?

2. Look carefully at the motives which cause us to be insincere in our relationships with people and in our prayers to God.

3. If we are sincere, we ought to be able to speak freely in a church fellowship without fear. Are there any constraints, however, which we ought to recognise?

4. I once heard it said that we recognise and like in Jesus those qualities which give us in our own lives most self-satisfaction. Is that true or could the opposite be true, that we admire in Jesus just what we lack in ourselves?

5. Do you find it difficult to be completely honest in your prayers?

6. Is 'economy with the truth' a necessity in a) social life, b) in politics?

7. Some churches advise their members to avoid the company of unbelievers and men and women of a sinful way of life, and in consequence tend to look down from a height at the sinful world. Jesus, by contrast, lived among 'publicans and sinners'. Discuss the pros and cons of this.

SESSION 10

The Mission of Reconciliation

For he is our peace, in his flesh he has made both groups into one and has broken down the dividing wall, that is, the hostility between us.

Ephesians 2:14

And the cause of peace like most other causes has often been ill served by its advocates . . . An ideal of safety, comfort and prosperity is not one that appeals to the finest characters.

F. R. Barry, *The Relevance of Christianity*

The Beatitude: Blessed are the peacemakers, for they shall be called the children of God.

The biblical idea of peace

For us today the word peacemaker conjures up visions of diplomats and special envoys like Cyrus Vance and Lord Owen struggling to find a peace plan for the former Yugoslavia. The older of us may perhaps look back to Dag Hammerskold, who died in the midst of his reconciling work as Secretary to the United Nations.

Peace, and therefore the role of the peacemaker, was different in the biblical world. Peace included the ending of strife and war, but it had a much wider application. Peace meant wholeness and health, soundness and well being. It applied as much to the individual as to the community. To have peace was to be sound in health and conscious of well being. It was the gift of God, not a state or condition to be achieved by diplomacy or other human design. 'Shalom', the Hebrew word for peace, was a word of greeting. It expressed both the peaceable intentions of the two who greeted each other, and conveyed an unspoken prayer for mutual health, wholeness and well being.

Although this may seem foreign to our ears, in fact it corresponds very closely to the nature of the life of the universe. The physical world exhibits two contrary principles, of attraction and repulsion. It can be seen in magnetism, where unlike poles in the magnet attract and like poles repel. It is the principle of attraction which promotes life, and is the channel of reproduction throughout the natural world. By contrast the splitting of the atom is a source of highly dangerous and potentially destructive power. The human body exhibits the same tendencies. Lesions are apt to be the seat of growths. Psychological and mental lesions cause personality disturbances. By contrast we know that where there is a unity of bodily, mental and spiritual activity there is wholeness, the personality being drawn together in peace.

We hardly need to note the disastrous consequences where, in a family, repulsion between man and wife replaces the original attraction which led to marriage. Nor need we dwell on the calamitous effects of splintering nationalisms and tribal

47

passions. They shout at us every day from television and newspaper. The absence of peace is in fact absence of health and wholeness whether in a home, in a nation, or in a whole continent.

So in the biblical sense the peacemaker is the bridge builder, the author and channel of wholeness, a person committed to the mission of reconciliation.

Jesus the peacemaker

Jesus was the peacemaker par excellence. The quotation from Ephesians at the head of this study says as much. But we shall only understand both his role, and that which he blesses, by glancing back once more at the Old Testament.

The inheritance of Jesus

The idea of peace was central to the Jewish faith. The Covenant which God made with his people was a covenant of life and peace (Mal. 2:5). God's thoughts were thoughts of peace which he would communicate to his people (Jer. 29:11 and Ps. 85:8). In consequence God requires peace of his people (Zech. 8:16 and Ps. 34:14). They are 'to seek peace and pursue it'. There will be no peace without righteousness, but righteousness will bring peace:

> The effect of righteousness will be peace, and the result of righteousness, quietness and trust forever. My people will abide in a peaceful habitation, in secure dwellings, and in quiet resting places.
>
> Isaiah 32:17-18

It is the same prophet who tells us that the Messiah will be the Prince of Peace (Is. 9:6). His namesake during the Exile tells us, however, that peace is costly. The servant of God suffered, and 'the chastisement of our peace was upon him, and with his stripes we are healed.' The Second Isaiah also gives voice to a well known verse which is closely related to the Beatitude.

> How beautiful upon the mountains are the feet of him that bringeth good tidings, that publisheth peace.
>
> Isaiah 52:7

Jesus, the reconciling Son of God

Jesus was the Reconciler, as Paul says in 2 Corinthians 5:19: 'God was in Christ reconciling the world to himself.' It was as the Son of God that he was able to build the bridge across the chasm which men had created between themselves and God – and in consequence between themselves.

This is important for our understanding of the Beatitude, because those who become peacemakers or reconcilers share in the same relationship with God. They will be called children of God, or as the NEB puts it, 'God shall call them his sons.' So to share in the costly work of reconciliation and making peace is to share in the greatest blessing, to be children of God or sons of God, to share in Christ's blessing in a special way.

Such men and women require first of all the gift of peace for, as the author of Hebrews puts it, without peace no man shall see the Lord. Both Paul's Epistles and John's gospel speak of that gift of peace. In Romans 5:1 Paul explains that God has brought peace to us through the cross, by which we are reconciled to God. In Romans 15:13 he says that peace is God's gift to those who have faith. John twice records Jesus' promise of the gift of peace, (John 14:27 and 16:33) whilst in the post resurrection story of the Upper Room, Jesus gives his disciples his peace through the gift of the Holy Spirit. It is this gift which makes it possible for the role of peacemaker to be played by vulnerable and imperfect human beings.

The peacemaker in action

There are a number of aspects of the role of peacemaker, and a number of activities which might warrant describing a person as a peacemaker.

The man or woman who, either by preaching or by a caring role in the church, seeks to draw others into communion with God in Christ is a peacemaker, even if their work does not seem very obvious. Paul says that we have been entrusted with a ministry of reconciliation, and that means that we must seek to effect a reconciliation between people who have been alienated from God, or who have lost sight of him. It is not an easy role, because many churchgoing people do not see the role of the preacher in that light. That he should offer food for thought on spiritual and moral issues, give shape to their weekly self-examination and moral stock taking, reassure them in times of uncertainty or suffering, seems to be the fulfilment of what they expect. That he should plead for penitence, for a commitment to Christ which involves being reconciled to God, might seem startling to many.

The active aspect is more obvious. The Christian who devotes his or her energies to ecumenical projects or local inter-church relationships is recognised, if not always welcomed. The peacemaker trying to intervene between mutually suspicious denominations has been a twentieth century spiritual hero, through whom God has drawn Christians into greater mutual sympathy and understanding. I find it almost miraculous that I should be able to share a service in my own church with both a Roman Catholic and an Anglican priest, when I consider the uneasy and even hostile relationships between those churches in my Lancashire boyhood. There is a long way to go before we can feel that the bitter past is absolutely dead, but the change thus far has been quite revolutionary.

A great deal of reconciling activity is secular, of course. The work of the United Nations and of neutral diplomats who seek to prevent disputes from erupting into violence is peacemaking of a high order, for which as Christians we should not simply be grateful, but help to create the kind of moral environment in which it has a chance of success. We ought also to pay attention to the efforts of quite ordinary people who, in places like Northern Ireland, seek to allay irrational fears and combat prejudice across the bitter sectarian divisions. Church leaders do play their part in political reconciliation in many parts of the world, in South Africa for instance. They need the courageous support of ordinary Christians.

At a family level the work of Relate is that of a reconciling agency, carried out with great tact and skill. Once more Christians are deeply involved as individuals in this work, but it is a secular agency. There was a time when the local priest or minister might have been the one who attempted to reconcile the members of a disrupted family. Today it falls to Relate and to social workers. It might be worth asking ourselves whether the Church still has a part to play, if only by sustaining those who are in the front line.

Some reflections

The task of the peacemakers can be a thankless one. They are too often caught in the middle of bitterness and rancour for which they have no responsibility. They face accusations of lack of principle from both sides, especially from those hard-liners who are unprepared to accept anything but outright victory for their cause. This was noticeable quite recently in Ireland when Senator Wilson, whose daughter had been killed in the bomb explosion at Enniskillen, and whose immediate expression of forgiveness for the perpetrators had moved the world to hushed respect, tried to stretch out a hand to the IRA. He was immediately vilified by hard-liners as being lacking in principle, foolish or improperly interfering in what was not his business. It is a very common experience for peacemakers.

There is also fear lest the peacemaker should succeed. Too many vested interests are involved. Some leaders in a serious dispute would find themselves relegated to oblivion if it were resolved and the parties reconciled. It is in their interests to prolong the strife, and they above all hate the peacemaker. He is, for them, an interfering busybody.

Being a peacemaker entails very distinctive qualities of character. A hot tempered or sarcastic peacemaker is a contradiction in terms. So is an impatient one. They who seek peace must speak peace.

It is noticeable that all the qualities which Jesus blessed are needed by the peacemaker. In that sense this Beatitude is rightly at the apogee of blessings. For instance, an arrogant person would not stand a chance. Nor would a person who lacked human sympathy, who did not recognise the genuine hurt and grievance which were helping to cause the dispute. A man who took himself too seriously or who lacked the serenity to take rebuffs without loss of faith and hope, in fact who lacked meekness, would have little chance of success. So would the person who was careless about justice and fairness, who had not passion for right. Few would trust the peacemaker who proved to be insincere, who was not pure in heart in that sense. Just as Jesus himself is the sum of all the qualities of the Beatitudes, and is the great reconciler, so the reconciling peacemaker needs the qualities of Christ. There can scarcely be a more demanding role for the Christian.

Questions

1. It is sometimes pointed out that the words of Jesus seem contradictory. He said that he would give peace to his disciples, but also that he came not to bring peace, but a sword. Can you reconcile these statements?

2. If we think of peace as wholeness in the biblical sense, which particular people in their professional roles are peacemakers?

3. Does the Church give adequate support to reconciling agencies both at the domestic and political level?

4. Peace at the end of a dispute usually means compromise. What principles should the peacemaker heed in seeking acceptance?

5. Has the Church any direct part to play as a peacemaker in domestic and industrial strife, or is it best left to the professional?

6. Is it true that sometimes those who work for peace can be its worst enemies because of their character and tactics?

7. Which of the qualities blessed by Jesus in the Beatitudes do you consider most necessary to the peacemaker?

8. If to be a peacemaker is a costly matter, what do you think is the greatest cost the peacemaker must bear?

SESSION 11

The Christian in a Hostile World

A religion which is perfectly at home in the world has no counsel for it which the world could not gain by an easier method.

R. Niebuhr, *Does Civilisation need Religion?*

The Beatitude: Blessed are they which are persecuted for righteousness sake, for theirs is the Kingdom of Heaven. Blessed are ye when men shall revile you, and persecute you, and shall say all manner of evil against you falsely for my sake. Rejoice, and be exceeding glad, for great is your reward in heaven.

The nature of religious persecution

Religious persecution is an oft-recurring phenomenon. It may occur where there is violent religious conflict and one religious body either controls or strongly influences the government of a state. This happened in sixteenth century Europe. In England three of the Tudors persecuted Catholics, and the fourth, Mary, persecuted Protestants. It may also occur when a secular state, for its own reasons, persecutes Christians or other religious people. This has occurred in Communist countries in our own time. A fictional example can be seen in Graham Greene's novel *The Power and the Glory*.

The young Christian Church successively faced both kinds of persecution. In the early days the Jewish authorities through the unconverted Saul of Tarsus sought to destroy Christian influence. When Paul, the persecutor turned apostle, began to preach the gospel and teach among the Jewish communities in Asia Minor and Greece, they attacked him. By the time the epistles of Peter were written the Roman Empire had become the much more powerful persecutor and it was Nero and some of his successors who tried unsuccessfully to destroy the Christian Church.

Why persecution occurs

A religious body may adopt one of two stances in its relationship with society. It may accept a position as a national or imperial church. This happened in the fourth century AD when Constantine declared Christianity to be the official religion of the Roman Empire. After the collapse of the Roman Empire, the Church had a chequered existence until the end of the first millennium. Then with the crowning of Charlemagne as Holy Roman Emperor, Christianity once more became the official religion of Western Europe.

On both occasions the effect was the same. The Church compromised and accepted society as it was with much of its violence and barbarism in exchange for the hope that it might influence the life of the world around it. To its credit it did succeed in softening some of the harshness, in securing greater justice, and for a time the rulers even of the most powerful states held the Church in considerable respect, and were loth to offend it.

Inevitably there were those who complained of the worldliness of the Church. Some, with the full approval of the Church, retreated into monastic life, preserving the discipline and devotion which seemed to have been lost. But from time to time there were rebellions when groups of Christians tried to turn the clock back to an earlier age.

That earlier position, which was that of the New Testament churches, left the Church as a relatively small, highly disciplined group of people, strict in their moral life, uncompromising in their beliefs and highly critical of the society about them. This was always more likely to provoke persecution. When Christian priests and prophets spoke out against evil rulers, or attacked the common practices of the wealthy and powerful, they were resented. Because they owed allegiance to Christ, their loyalty to the state was suspect. It was not difficult for demagogues to whip up mob hysteria.

Thus, for example, from the sixteenth century onwards until our own time, Roman Catholics were wrongly suspected of disloyalty. In the late seventeenth century wild attacks on Roman Catholics occurred in London, and a hundred years later the Gordon Riots had the same purpose. The early Methodists were also suspected of having sympathy with Bonnie Prince Charlie and this accounts for the number of Methodist chapels which Wesley christened with names like Hanover and Brunswick, as a sign of loyalty to the ruling dynasty.

Secular persecution

Persecution, however, may occur which has little to do with the attitudes of the religious body itself. An unscrupulous ruler or government, faced with discontent in the country, may need a scapegoat in order to shift blame from its own shoulders. A religious body whose way of life and worship is something of a mystery and is therefore subject to prejudice and misunderstanding is an easy target.

Modern governments have often used latent anti-Semitism in this way. That few people have known much about Jewish worship and the Jewish way of life has made it all the easier, while the suspicion that they have undue influence through their financial power is easily fostered. One of the tragedies of mid-century Germany was the way in which German Christians were prepared to accept well dressed political lies about the Jews as a justification for Hitler's racial policies. Yet that is only a terrifying and violently extreme example of what has been a common occurrence elsewhere.

The young Church in peril

Given this background there is nothing particularly prophetic in the words of Jesus. Within Judaism the prophets had been persecuted, as Jesus pointed out both in the Sermon on the Mount (Matt. 5:12) and in the parable of the wicked husbandmen. (Mark 12:1-12). The claim of the Christian preachers that the Jewish authorities had actually crucified the Messiah and the Son of God was sufficient to guarantee persecution and violent opposition in the synagogues throughout Palestine, Asia Minor and Greece, the story of which is contained in the Acts of the Apostles.

The Acts also make it clear that, for a time at least, Paul met a degree of friendliness from the Roman authorities wherever he went. At Philippi his Roman citizenship

53

caused panic among the magistrates (Acts 16:37f). At Corinth the Roman governor Gallio refused to listen to Jewish complaints against Paul (Acts 18:12f). When eventually Paul returned to Palestine, the Roman authorities saved his life, when a conspiracy was hatched which would have had him ambushed on the way to Caesarea (Acts 23:12f). And although Paul spent some months in prison in Caesarea, he was treated quite kindly, was able to receive his friends and to communicate without hindrance with the churches (Acts 24 and 25).

Part of the reason for this lay in Paul's Roman citizenship, but at first there was little disposition to persecute Christians at all, because they were regarded as a Jewish sect. It was only when the Roman authorities discerned that much greater claims were being made for Christ as the Son of God, who had a universal claim to the obedience and service of mankind, that a more hostile attitude took the place of the earlier tolerance. After all, the Emperor was regarded as divine and as having a prior claim to the worship of all the peoples of the Roman Empire, except the Jews who were tactfully excluded. Christians preaching such a universal gospel could not claim the same immunity from worshipping the Emperor. Their loyalty was suspect and they became a convenient target for persecution.

Some reflections

The relationship of the Church to the society in which it stands is always a sensitive issue. For instance, the closer relationships of the Church of England with other denominations and the critical attitude of Anglican leaders towards some government policies today has raised the issue in fairly acute form, giving rise to a desire in some quarters for disestablishment of the Church of England.

This raises some searching questions. Can the Church ever be truly Christian if it acts as a moral prop to a secular society? Will there not be times when it is led into giving God's blessing to practices which are clearly contrary to the Christian faith? Is this not particularly acute in wartime? Moreover is it not wrong that, because of its established status, appointments in the Church should involve political leaders who do not profess the Christian faith? Is not the Church severely handicapped in its ability to speak critically of the national government, and of moral and social evils in society? And where its leaders do so, is it not all too easy for the threat of political interference to emerge in order to secure more complacent Church leaders?

On the other hand does not a sect forfeit its right to speak to the nation in the name of God? Nonconformists would deny this and claim that the very independence of the dissenting churches enables them to speak more freely. Some, indeed, would argue that established churches are too comfortable in society (to quote Niebuhr), and that Christians must be free to risk persecution and the penalties of the law, if they are to be both true to Christ and effective in evangelism and witness.

Some Christians would take the view of course that passive obedience to authority is the only correct attitude for the Christian and would cite Paul's words in Romans 13:1:

> Let every person be subject to the governing authorities; for there is no authority except from God, and those authorities that exist have been instituted by God. Therefore whoever resists authority resists what God has appointed and those who resist will incur judgment.

The same direction is given by the author of the first Epistle of Peter 2:13:

> For the Lord's sake accept the authority of every human institution . . . For it is God's will that by doing right you should silence the ignorance of the foolish.

The motive here is clearly to avoid suspicion of disloyalty, even though the author takes a less exalted view of authority than Paul. It is man-made, not derived from God.

St. Augustine, in his *City of God*, followed Paul in demanding strict obedience, and there has always been a strand in Christian thinking down the centuries which refused to countenance any act of civil disobedience, however passive or non-violent. Even Dietrich Bonhoeffer in his *Ethics* could only justify opposition to the state where it interfered with the teaching of the Church. In fact he was not always consistent, and did advocate sticking 'a spoke in the wheel' of the Hitler government in defence of the Jews, but theoretically he believed rigidly in obedience. There is much to ponder here.

In what is now called the post-Christian world, it is not impossible that there will arise from time to time governments in most countries which are hostile to the Christian faith. Persecution may occur without any overt acts of opposition from the Church. It may be very subtle, taking the form of discrimination, as well as more legal restriction of worship or the dissemination of belief. Then Christians would be faced with a choice of some magnitude, whether to accept the status of a pietist sect, deprived of the liberty to preach, possibly deprived of economic or civil liberties, or to risk more violent persecution for the sake of the gospel which has been committed to its hands.

Questions

1. Do you regard the Church as embracing all men and women as children of God, or as a body of highly dedicated and disciplined Christians at odds with the unChristian society around them?

2. If the Church is to influence the moral character of the society in which it stands, is this best achieved a) by pressing for stricter laws, b) by trying to use the media to promote Christian morality, c) by the example of Christians living in the community?

3. Look at the forms of persecution open to a government today. Which of the following do you think would be most difficult to counter and to endure? a) exclusion from professions, b) discrimination against Christian children, c) discrimination in matters of housing, health services and education, d) exclusion of Christians from the media.

4. Anti-semitism is a prevalent disease today. Try to analyse its causes, and see if there are ways in which the Church can counteract the prejudice and its expressions.

5. Do you agree with Bonhoeffer's view that Christians ought to oppose the authority of the state only if it seeks to corrupt the teaching of the Church?

6. Are there issues on which the Christian ought to take a conscientious stand against authority even if it means incurring the penalties of the law?

7. Are we active enough in our support for those who are persecuted?

8. Is the state a divine authority as Paul suggests, or is it man-made as 1 Peter 2 implies?

SESSION 12

Channels of Blessing

> The Christian Ethic is not a selfish thing, but must be adopted for the sake of the world in general. The aim is not to acquire merit, but to distribute blessing.
>
> T. H. Robinson, *The Moffat Commentary on Matthew's Gospel*

Passage for study: Matthew 5:13-16

A gospel in metaphors

These three verses, though not Beatitudes, belong to the train of thought which Jesus was pursuing. The Beatitudes have all pointed away from self-centredness towards God and our neighbour. These verses confirm that the vocation of the Christian, and of the Church, is to serve Christ in the world, and to serve the world for Christ. As Robinson says, we are not Christians because that makes us more commendable, or even because it makes us feel good, but because we are called to serve.

There is something of a contrast between the two metaphors which Jesus uses here. Salt is an essential but inconspicuous element in our daily lives. Unless we have used it, we do not taste the salt in our food. The salt simply calls attention to the taste of the food itself. Light, by contrast, illuminates our whole life, whether it floods into our morning as we draw back the curtains, or blazes from the signs in Piccadilly Circus. Natural or artificial, primitive or ultramodern, we are sensitively conscious of its changing pattern and intensity, of its presence and absence. And that contrast is essential to the teaching of Jesus here.

Salt

Salt in the Bible

Common salt is ubiquitous. In Palestine its source was the Dead Sea where there was a seven mile length of solid rock salt. Until modern refrigeration technology took over, salt was essential to the preservation of food, especially meat. Even today it is used in some parts of the food industry. It is also valuable as an antiseptic, and was so used in ancient times, without the reason for the healing process necessarily being understood.

Among Eastern peoples, and Semitic peoples in particular, salt is the symbol of fidelity and friendship. To have taken a man's salt, that is to have been entertained in his home, was to be under a bond of faithfulness and trust to him. The Old Testament, too, has instances where the phrase 'covenant of salt' is used. The word salt gives an added seriousness to the obligation which the covenant laid upon those who were bound by it. This is probably the meaning of the saying which Jesus adds to Matthew's version of this verse in Mark 9:50:

> Have salt in yourselves, and be at peace with one another.

57

There is a bond between them which demands the seriousness associated with salt, and which they must observe, living at peace with each other.

The teaching of Jesus

In the verse we are studying, therefore, we should remember this element of seriousness and steadfastness. The Christian may be unobtrusive like salt, but in his steadfastness he will bring qualities to the life of the world about him, which will help him to deserve the description 'salt of the earth'.

A man who is steadfast in his compassion, who by his forgiveness enables another to make a new start, who shares the grief which is crushing a neighbour, or who unremittingly seeks justice for the poor, the hungry and the oppressed, will bring out qualities in the lives of other people which have been submerged by sin, or sorrow, or privation. The Christian will not have called attention to himself, but like salt will have released the latent riches in the lives of others. The qualities of the Beatitudes act like salt in giving savour to the life of the world.

Likewise the activities of those who passionately seek justice, or at cost to themselves work for peace at whatever level, may be inconspicuous and unknown, yet they constitute the real protection of the world against evil. Like salt they are an antiseptic. In the same way it could be said that the Christian Church should be a preserving agency, ensuring that the moral and spiritual achievements of humanity are not lost. Perhaps it is one argument in favour of preserving great cathedrals and cherishing fine Church music by training cathedral choirs, that what men and women have accomplished in the past to the glory of God is not lost.

A reflection

But has the Church sometimes failed to be the salt of the earth? When Christians have indulged in persecution, or their bitter differences have led to social discrimination, hatred and even open war, has its action been either antiseptic against evil or preservative of good? In an article, T. Gorringe the chaplain of St. John's College, Oxford, lamenting so much communal strife could write:

> But here, as in other parts of the world, religion seems to be part of the disease rather than the cure.

And later he concludes that it is 'Christian communalism which calls in question the unity we are supposed to embody.' The history of religious intolerance does more today to keep many decent and thoughtful people out of the Church than any other single cause.

Yet there is no other source of a gospel of forgiveness which can release men from the grip of evil on their lives. Nor is there in the world a faith which so relies upon the power of love to authenticate its message. And although there are many who do not accept the Christian belief in God or Christ, who dedicate themselves to the service of the vulnerable and broken, it is questionable how long such service could survive the passing of the Christian faith. There are already signs of a drying up of compassion for the aged, the mentally ill and the deprived, which, in my view, is a long term effect of the decline in Christian influence.

So the Church must keep its 'savour', its love. It has nothing else to offer. There is no sophisticated philosophy of life. There is no Christian political programme as such. We offer love and if that fails then we are only 'fit to be cast out and trodden under foot of men'. What a dire warning and what a responsibility!

Light

The biblical basis

It is no accident that the first command of God in Genesis 1 is 'let there be light', because without light life is unthinkable. In Job 10:22 the total absence of light means death:

> Let me alone, that I may find a little comfort before I go, never to return, to the land of gloom and deep darkness, the land of gloom and chaos, where light is like darkness.

Because light is a first essential for life, it was seen as the first attribute of God himself. Psalm 104:2 describes God as covering himself 'with light as with a garment'. So to have light is to have the blessing of God. For the blessed 'the light shall shine upon all thy ways' (Job 22:28). Light, too, is a principal ingredient of the promises of God. For instance, in Isaiah 9:2 the familiar words read:

> The people that walked in darkness have seen a great light; they that dwell in the land of the shadow of death, upon them hath the light shined.

In the later prophets and in the 'wisdom' literature, such as Proverbs, light has a moral quality:

> But the path of the righteous is like the light of dawn, which shines brighter and brighter until full day.
>
> Proverbs 4:18

It is this moral quality which is carried into the New Testament, both as an attribute of God himself, and as expressing the moral life of man. Thus the first Epistle of John proclaims that 'God is Light and in him there is no darkness at all.' That this is a moral quality is made clear when he goes on to say:

> But if we walk in the light as he himself is in the light we have fellowship with one another.
>
> 1 John 1:7

By implication to be indwelt by God's love is to live in the light. Clearly this catches the sense of the word of Jesus himself.

Jesus, the Light of the World

If God is Light, it is not surprising to find that Jesus is spoken of as the Light of the World. In the Nunc Dimittis (Luke 2:32) the child Jesus is referred to as 'a light to lighten the Gentiles and the glory of my people Israel'. The Fourth Evangelist makes much of the idea.

Thus in John 1:4:

> What has come into being in him was life, and the life was the light of all people. The light shines in the darkness, and the darkness did not overcome it.

Again in John 9:5 Jesus says:

> As long as I am in the world, I am the light of the world.

Then in John 12:46:

> I have come as light into the world, so that everyone who believes in me should not remain in the darkness.

Thus when Jesus spoke of his disciples as being the light of the world he was implying that their task was to be a continuing source of the light that he himself had brought.

The Church – the Light of the World

We may find a deeper understanding of Jesus' words by looking at the Epistles, which clearly echo the same thought whilst expanding it. In Colossians 1:12 Paul congratulates his readers because they 'are privileged to share the lot of those who are living in the light'. He is suggesting that they have found a way of life which is both redeeming and enabling. They are saved from their sins and by the gift of the Spirit endowed with moral energy. So when Jesus tells his disciples to let their light shine in the world, he is implying that their lives must lead men and women to discover the redeeming grace which is theirs.

In Ephesians 5:8f Paul emphasises the moral character of light:

> Live as children of light, for the fruit of the light is found in all that is good and right and true. Try to find out what is pleasing to the Lord. Take no part in the unfruitful works of darkness, but instead expose them.

If this had been a commentary on the words of Jesus it could scarcely have been a better explanation. Christians are privileged to share the work of Jesus in the world and to shed his light abroad by their moral example.

Jesus himself emphasises the importance of fearless Christian living. Christians are not to hide their allegiance. Light is meant to enlighten, not to be hidden. An uncompromising witness without flamboyant exhibitionism seems to be implied. The light is to be a quietly useful domestic lamp, not a football ground floodlight. We are to be faithful in our limited but essential role.

The last words of the passage sum up the teaching of Jesus. The end of all human life is the glory of God, to demonstrate the infinite worth of his love in the world. The qualities which we have examined in these studies do just that. They are reflections of the character of God himself, of his compassion, of his zeal for justice, of his reaching out to us in Jesus that we might have peace, and of his transparent holiness. In this way alone and by these qualities alone can we display for all to see the worth of the God we worship, and the Master we serve.

Questions

1. Think together of some of the ways in which the life and witness of the Church and of individual Christians can counteract evil.

2. Examine some of the ways in which the Church has preserved what is best in human life and endeavour down the ages.

3. Discuss the words of the Oxford College chaplain. Do the failures of the churches neutralise the good?

4. Is there any political programme which can be said to be Christian?

5. What do you understand by the words of Jesus, 'I am the Light of the World'?

6. 'Quiet example rather than public profession is the best way of witness for the individual Christian.' Do you agree?

7. 'The chief end of man is to glorify God and to enjoy him for ever.' What do you understand by these words from the Anglican Catechism? Do you agree with them?

ACKNOWLEDGEMENTS

The following copyright material has been used by kind permission of the publishers.

Front cover: Lake Derwent Water, photographed by Susan Hibbins.

page 3, 48   F. R. Barry, *The Relevance of Christianity*, James Nisbet & Co. Ltd

page 3   Iris Murdoch, *The Sovereignty of the Good*, Routledge

page 6, 40   T. W. Manson, *The Teaching of Jesus*, Cambridge University Press

page 7, 29   T. S. Eliot, *Selected Prose*, Faber and Faber Ltd

page 17   Bryn Rees, *The kingdom of God* (HP139), Mrs O. A. Scott

page 30, 34, 37, 58
    T. H. Robinson, *The Moffat Commentary on Matthew's Gospel*, Hodder & Stoughton

page 34   Philip Watson, *Let God be God*, Epworth Press

Every effort has been made to trace copyright owners, but where we have been unsuccessful we would welcome information which would enable us to make appropriate acknowledgement in any reprint.